simply pasta

A STUNNING COLLECTION OF 140 PASTA AND NOODLE DISHES FOR ALL OCCASIONS SHOWN IN MORE THAN 200 MOUTHWATERING PHOTOGRAPHS

valerie ferguson

southwater

This edition is published by Southwater, an imprint of Anness Publishing Ltd, Hermes House, 88–89 Blackfriars Road, London SE1 8HA; tel. 020 7401 2077; fax 020 7633 9499

www.southwaterbooks.com; www.annesspublishing.com

UK distributor: Book Trade Services; tel. 0116 2759086; fax 0116 2759090; uksales@booktradeservices.com; exportsales@booktradeservices.com
North American distributor: National Book Network; tel. 301 459 3366; fax 301 429 5746; www.nbnbooks.com
Australian distributor: Pan Macmillan Australia; tel. 1300 135 113; fax 1300 135 103; customer.service@macmillan.com.au
New Zealand distributor: David Bateman Ltd; tel. (09) 415 7664; fax (09) 415 8892

Publisher: Joanna Lorenz
Editor: Valerie Ferguson
Designer: Carole Perks
Typesetter: Diane Pullen
Editorial Reader: Richard McGinlay
Production Controller: Claire Rae

Recipes contributed by:
Catherine Atkinson, Alex Barker, Michelle Berriedale-Johnson, Angela Boggiano, Janet Brinkworth, Carla Capalbo, Kit Chan, Jacqueline Clark, Maxine Clarke, Frances Cleary, Trish Davies, Roz Denny, Patrizia Diemling, Matthew Drennan, Sarah Edmonds, Rafi Fernandez, Christine France, Sarah Gates, Shirley Gill, Nicola Graimes, Rosamund Grant, Rebekah Hassan, Deh-Ta Hsuing, Shehzad Husain, Christine Ingram, Judy Jackson, Masaki Ko, Lesley Mackley, Norma MacMillan, Sue Maggs, Kathy Man, Elizabeth Martin, Sallie Morris, Annie Nichols, Maggie Pannell, Katherine Richmond, Anne Sheasby, Jenny Stacey, Liz Trigg, Hilaire Walden, Laura Washburn, Steven Wheeler, Judy Williams and Jeni Wright

Photographers:
William Adams-Lingwood, Karl Adamson, Edward Allwright, David Armstrong, Steve Baxter, Micki Dowie, James Duncan, John Freeman, Ian Garlick, Michelle Garrett, John Heseltine, Amanda Heywood, Janine Hosegood, David Jordan, Don Last, Patrick McLeavey, Thomas Odulate, Juliet Piddington and Peter Reilly

ETHICAL TRADING POLICY

Because of our ongoing ecological investment programme, you, as our customer, can have the pleasure and reassurance of knowing that a tree is being cultivated on your behalf to naturally replace the materials used to make the book you are holding. The forests we manage contain more than 3.5 times the number of trees employed each year in making paper for the books we manufacture. For further information about this scheme, go to www.annesspublishing.com/trees

A CIP catalogue record for this book is available from the British Library.

Previously published as part of a larger volume, *500 Greatest-Ever Pasta Recipes*

NOTES

Bracketed terms are intended for American readers.
For all recipes, quantities are given in both metric and imperial measures and, where appropriate, in standard cups and spoons.
Follow one set of measures, but not a mixture, because they are not interchangeable.
Standard spoon and cup measures are level. 1 tsp = 5ml, 1 tbsp = 15ml, 1 cup = 250ml/8fl oz.
Australian standard tablespoons are 20ml. Australian readers should use 3 tsp in place of 1 tbsp for measuring small quantities.
American pints are 16fl oz/2 cups. American readers should use 20fl oz/2.5 cups in place of 1 pint when measuring liquids.
Electric oven temperatures in this book are for conventional ovens. When using a fan oven, the temperature will probably need to be reduced by about 10–20°C/20–40°F. Since ovens vary, you should check with your manufacturer's instruction book for guidance.
Medium (US large) eggs are used unless otherwise stated.
Main front cover image shows Spaghetti with Ham & Saffron – for recipe, see page 43.

PUBLISHER'S NOTE

Although the advice and information in this book are believed to be accurate and true at the time of going to press, neither the authors nor the publisher can accept any legal responsibility or liability for any errors or omissions that may have been made nor for any inaccuracies nor for any loss, harm or injury that comes about from following instructions or advice in this book.

simply
pasta

Contents

Introduction 6

Types of Pasta 8

Types of Noodle 11

Techniques 12

Soups & Salads 14

Quick & Easy 30

Midweek Meals 48

Vegetarian Pasta 64

Special Occasions 78

Index 94

Introduction

Easy to cook, economical, quick, convenient, healthy, satisfying, popular and so versatile that it goes with almost every other ingredient imaginable, pasta deserves a place in every kitchen. From midweek family suppers that need to be cooked virtually instantly to long summer lunches

to linger over with a glass of chilled wine, and from a simple, but classic vegetarian blend of cheese and cream to a magnificent dinner-party extravaganza of fresh shellfish and herbs, pasta is perfect for every occasion.

There are over 200 different pasta shapes – with about three times as many different names. Try topping curls, wheels, spirals, butterflies, shells or even "priest stranglers" with a vibrant mix of wild mushrooms and spicy sausage or a medley of sweet roasted vegetables. Envelop ribbons in a creamy coating of cheese and serve with prosciutto and asparagus, or bake pasta sheets, layered with a succulent meat and vegetables sauce, until golden brown and utterly irresistible. Little circles and squares can be filled with a piquant stuffing and served in a simple flavoured butter or an elegant consommé, while adding tiny stars, shells, thimbles and even alphabet shapes turns home-made soup into an appealing and substantial meal in a bowl.

This wealth of choice is only part of the picture, however. From Japanese buckwheat soba noodles to the ever-popular skeins of Chinese egg noodles, Asian cuisine also offers a prolific variety of fabulous dishes. Subtly spiced, with their characteristic harmony of flavours, colours and textures, these are soups, snacks, salads and suppers to delight family and friends and children and adults alike.

This inspirational collection of more than 140 recipes includes many traditional favourites,

yet even these are as diverse as Minestrone, Shellfish Chow Mein, Fettuccine all'Alfredo and Pork Meatballs with Pasta. Less familiar and contemporary dishes range from exquisite Japanese Summer Salad, served floating in bowls of iced water, to sumptuous Capelli d'Angelo with Lobster, cooked in sparkling wine – or champagne – and cream. Cook's tips and variations throughout the book offer helpful hints and extend your repertoire of mouthwatering pasta dishes. Five chapters – Soups & Salads, Quick & Easy, Midweek Meals, Vegetarian Pasta and Special Occasions – make it easy to find precisely the recipe you need. There are dishes that can be assembled in a matter of minutes from store-cupboard (pantry) ingredients, bakes you can prepare in advance and pop in the oven when you get home from work, flexible recipes that are easily adapted to match seasonal fresh produce, inexpensive, filling and easy family suppers and sophisticated and luxurious culinary treats for celebrations and dinner parties.

A useful introduction provides an illustrated guide to the most popular types of pasta and noodles. This is followed by a step-by-step techniques section, covering making pasta by hand and in a food processor. There are tips on using a pasta machine and also advice on shaping pasta by hand. Perhaps most important of all, is a guide to cooking perfect pasta every time, whether fresh or dried, filled or unfilled.

With *Simply Pasta* on the kitchen shelf, even the most inexperienced cook can conjure up a marvellous meal, even the busiest parent can make supper in moments and even the tightest budget can stretch to make food fit for a king. The only thing that isn't simple is the flavour.

Types of Pasta

The first forms of pasta were thin strings or ribbons, but it wasn't long before people started experimenting with shapes. Soon there were hundreds of these, often starting out as regional varieties, but spreading to the wider world. Today the range is enormous, and continues to grow. Shapes range from the beautiful to the bizarre. This book introduces a wide selection, but there's no need to limit yourself to our suggestions. Feel free to make substitutions, but bear in mind that long strands work best with thinner sauces, while short shapes are good with chunky, meaty sauces. Choose tubes or shells if you want to trap the sauce inside. Remember, too, that pasta names often vary from region to region.

Long Pasta

Bucatini looks like chunky spaghetti, but is hollow. **Bucatoni** is a fatter version, while **perciatelli** is bucatini by another name.

Capelli or **capelli d'angelo** translates as angel hair pasta, which is a fanciful name for this superfine pasta. It is often packed in nests – **capelli d'angelo a nidi**. **Capellini** are similar strands.

Chitarra is a square-shaped form of spaghetti, so named because it is made on a frame that resembles a guitar.

Fusilli lunghi, also known as **fusilli col buco**, are long twisted strands or spirals.

Linguine are slim ribbons. The name means "little tongues". This popular form of pasta is very good for serving with creamy coating sauces.

Macaroni (maccheroni) was one of the first shapes to be made, and remains very popular. Two short forms, the curved elbow macaroni and short-cut macaroni, are particularly widely used. A thin form of the long strands is **maccheroncini**.

Pappardelle are broad ribbon noodles, with either plain or wavy edges. **Trenette** are similar.

Spaghetti needs no introduction, but do try the less familiar forms, such as the skinny **spaghettini** or the flavoured **spaghetti con spinaci** (with spinach) or **spaghetti integrali** (whole-wheat).

Strangozzi is a thin noodle that is often sold as a loose plait. The basil flavour is delicious.

Tagliatelle is the most common form of ribbon noodle. It is sold in nests, which unravel on cooking. Several flavours – and therefore colours – are available, a popular mix being **paglia e fieno** (straw and hay) which consists of separate nests of egg noodles and spinach-flavoured noodles. The Roman version of tagliatelle is called **fettuccine**. **Tagliolini, tagliarini** and **fidelini** are thin ribbon noodles.

Vermicelli is very fine spaghetti.

Ziti is very long, thick and tubular, like macaroni, and is often broken into shorter lengths before being cooked.

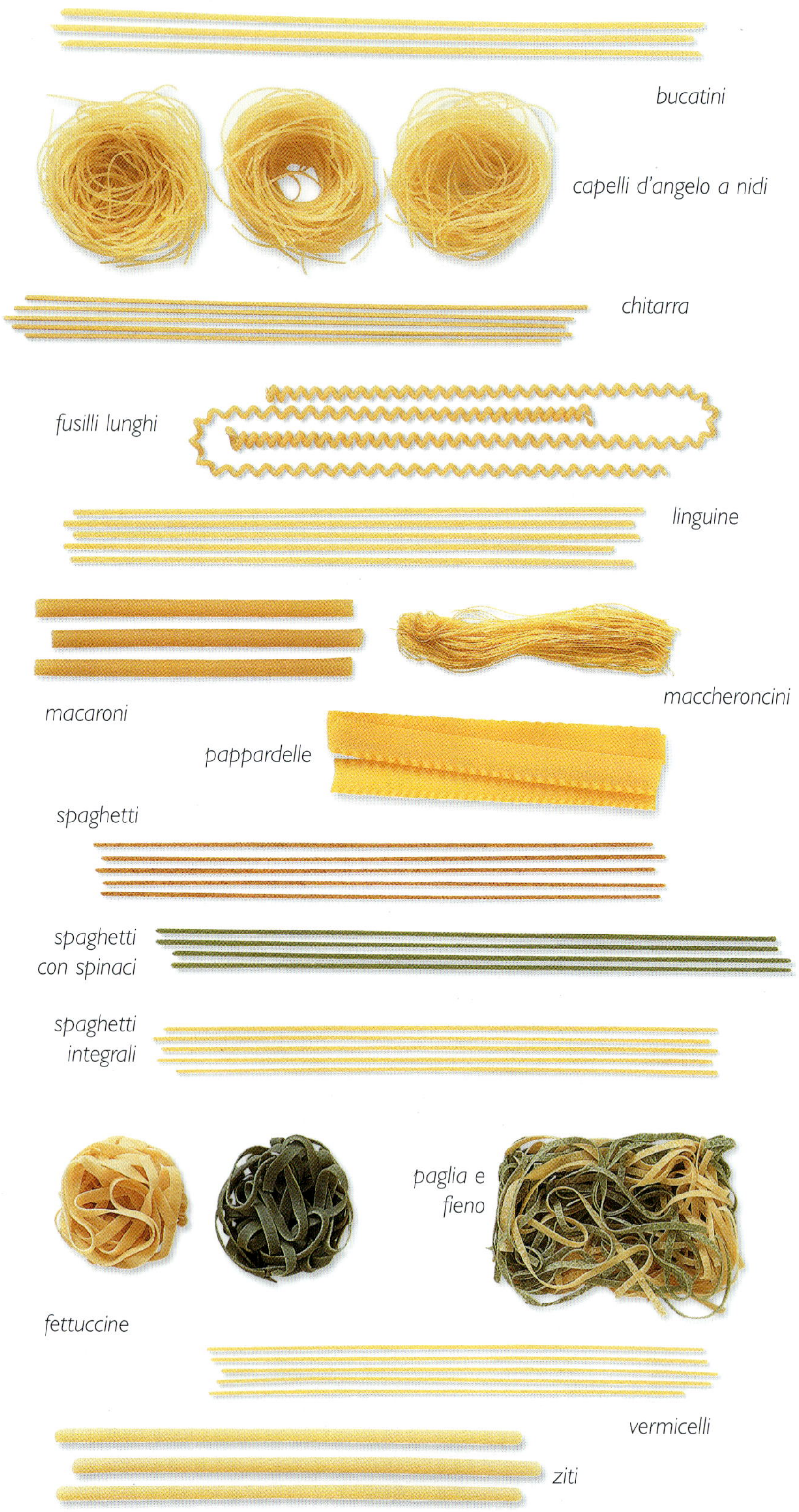

bucatini
capelli d'angelo a nidi
chitarra
fusilli lunghi
linguine
macaroni
maccheroncini
pappardelle
spaghetti
spaghetti con spinaci
spaghetti integrali
paglia e fieno
fettuccine
vermicelli
ziti

Short Pasta (Shapes)

Conchiglie are shells. Perfect for trapping sauces, they come in various sizes, from tiny **conchigliette** for soups to **conchiglione**, the jumbo shells which can be stuffed.

Eliche are among several spiral-shaped pastas, and resemble **fusilli** and **spirali** (which tend to be more open). They come in various thicknesses and flavours.

Farfalle are known in English as butterflies or bow-ties, which they resemble. They look very pretty on the plate, and are so popular that manufacturers produce several different varieties, including the ever-popular **farfalle tricolore**, which mixes plain or ridged red, green and yellow shapes.

Fiorelli These very pretty designer shapes look rather like oyster mushrooms, with frilly edges. They are not unlike the bell-shaped **campanelle**.

Fusilli are spirals, formed by winding fresh dough around a thin rod. They tend to relax and unwind a little when placed in boiling water.

Garganelli are a regional form of penne. Short and tubular, they look a little like scrolls, thanks to the special tool on which they are rolled. Called *il pettine*, this resembles a large comb.

Orecchiette are endearing small shapes, so named because they look like little ears. They are slightly chewy and are served with robust sauces.

Penne or quills are short lengths of tubular pasta which are cut on the slant so their ends are pointed. Sturdy and capable of holding sauces inside their hollow centres, they are deservedly popular. Both plain – **penne lisce** – and ridged versions – **penne rigate** – are available. **Rigatoni** are straight ridged tubes, somewhat fatter than penne.

Pipe are small pasta shapes. They don't resemble pipes, which is the translation of their Italian name, but are like small shells. **Pipe rigate** is the ridged version. They are available plain and wholemeal (whole-wheat).

Ruote or **Rotelle** are small wagon wheel shapes. They come in various flavours and colours, and are popular with children.

Strozzapreti sounds like such a pretty name. The word, however, means "priest stranglers", which is somewhat less attractive! Legend has it that the priest who originally tried them ate far too many and almost choked to death. Each shape consists of two slim strands of pasta that are twisted or "strangled" together.

conchiglie

conchiglione

eliche

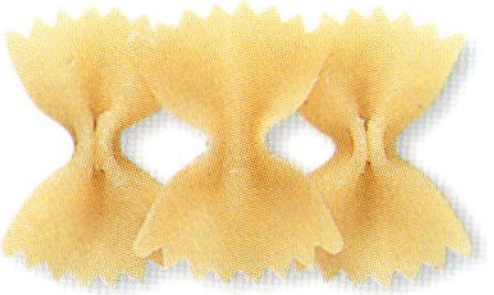
farfalle

farfalle tricolore

fiorelli

fusilli

garganelli

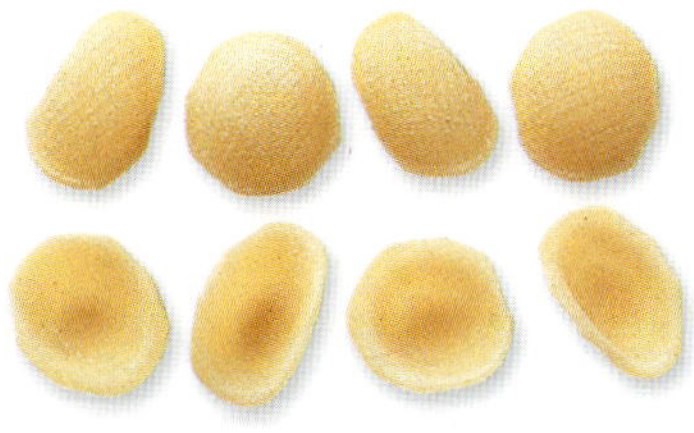
orecchiette

penne rigate

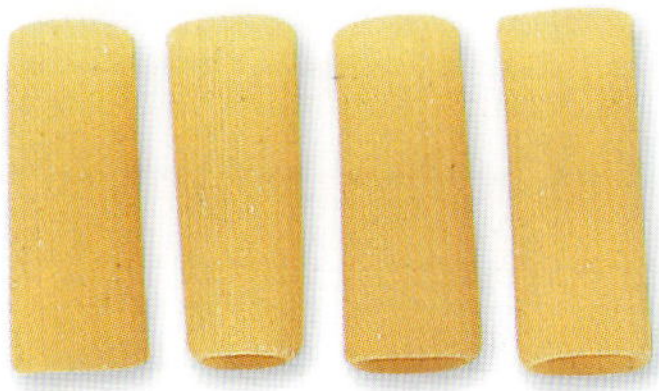
rigatoni

pipe rigate

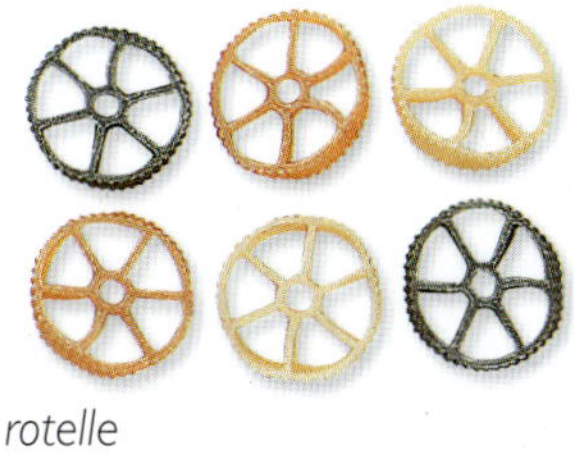
rotelle

strozzapreti

cannelloni

conchiglione

lasagne

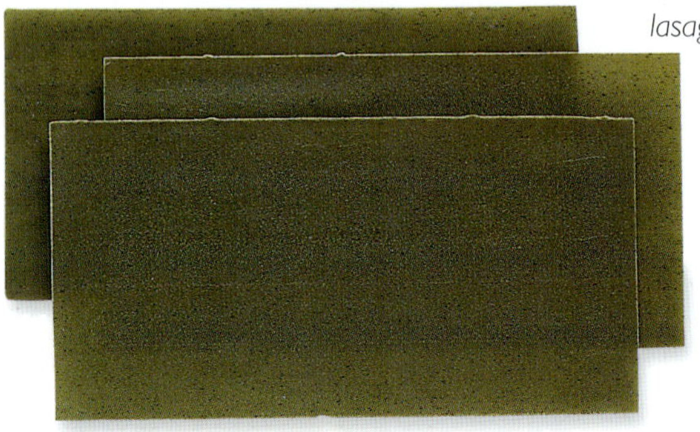
lasagne verdi

lasagnette

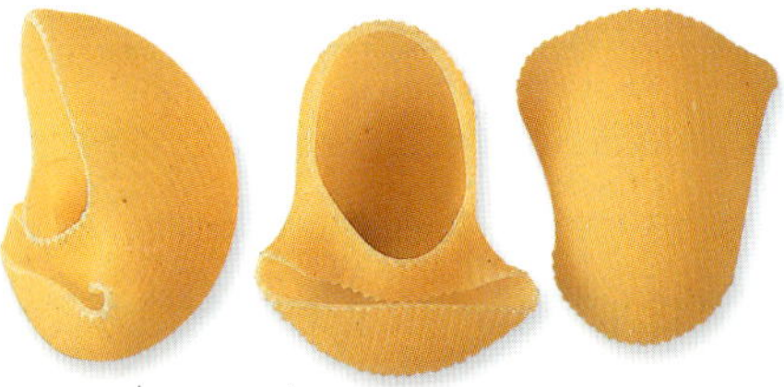
lumaconi

tortellini

ravioli

stellette

Pasta for Stuffing and Layering

Cannelloni About 10cm/4in in length, these large tubes are stuffed, coated in sauce and baked in the oven. In Italy, cannelloni are traditionally made by rolling fresh lasagne sheets around the filling, but the dried tubes are more convenient. Either pipe the filling in with a piping (pastry) bag, or use a teaspoon.

Conchiglione Jumbo pasta shells, these are wonderful for stuffing and look very pretty. They come in plain, spinach and tomato flavours, both smooth and ridged.

Lasagne This popular form of pasta comes in flat or wavy sheets, pre-cut for layering, and can be fresh or dried. There is also a no-precook version, which is very convenient, as it needs only to be layered with the sauce or sauces, and cooks as the dish bakes in the oven. There are some drawbacks with no-precook pasta – purists say it doesn't compare with other types in terms of taste, but as long as you buy a quality pasta, use more sauce than usual and cook the lasagne for at least 45 minutes, it gives a very good result. Sizes vary, so when you find one that fits your lasagne dish perfectly, it is well worth making a note of the manufacturer. You can snap sheets to fit, but they seldom break where you want them to. If you choose fresh or regular dried pasta, you will need to cook it before layering. Follow the instructions on the packet.

Flavoured lasagne Lasagne comes in several flavours, including green (spinach); brown (whole-wheat) and two tones of yellow, one being the plain lasagne and the other being the version with added egg.

Lasagnette are long, narrow strips of flat pasta, which are crimped on one or two sides. They are used in the same way as lasagne sheets.

Lumaconi These look a bit like large snail shells, with an opening at either end. They are awkward to stuff, but make an interesting change from more common shapes.

Filled Pasta

Fresh and dried filled pasta shapes are available. The range includes **ravioli** and **tortellini**, both of which can be served quite simply, with melted butter or a light sauce, and the lesser-known **agnolotti**, which look rather like round ravioli.

Pastina

These are miniature shapes, usually served in broth or soup. There are dozens of varieties, including **tubetti**, **stellette**, **risoni**, **peperini**, **ditalini** and **fregola**, which resembles couscous.

tubetti

Types of Noodle

Asian noodles are usually made from wheat, as is Italian pasta, but may also be made from rice, buckwheat, arrowroot or mung beans. The noodles are formed by various methods, the most dramatic of which is when the cook hurls pieces of dough into the air, twirling and twisting until they stretch and lengthen to form long, thin strands. In principle, the process is similar to that adopted by chefs when shaping pizza dough, but is even more impressive. There are many different types of noodle, some of which must be soaked in warm water before being cooked briefly – or just heated – in boiling water. Check the instructions on the packet, as timings can vary widely, but in general, the thinner the noodle, the less cooking it will need. In addition to being boiled, or heated in soups, noodles are an integral part of many vegetable dishes, and are often stir-fried or deep-fried. They may need to be boiled or soaked, then well drained, before frying.

Cellophane Noodles are made from ground mung beans, and are also known as bean thread, transparent or glass noodles. Although very thin, the strands are firm and resilient, and stay that way when cooked, never becoming soggy. Cellophane noodles are not served solo, but are added to soups or braised dishes.

Egg Noodles These can be fresh or dried, and come in various thicknesses, including fine, medium and broad. They are often packed in what look like skeins or coils, and the general rule is to use one of these per person. The Japanese equivalent are called **ramen**.

Rice Noodles come in several different forms and are usually sold in bundles. The very thin white ones are called **rice vermicelli**. These cook almost instantly when added to hot broth, provided they have first been soaked in warm water.

Soba Noodles Japanese buckwheat noodles, these often include wheat flour and/or yam flour. They are much darker in colour than regular wheat noodles and are sold in bundles.

Somen Noodles also come from Japan and are made from wheat starch. Thin and delicate, they are sold in bundles tied with a paper band.

Udon Noodles are plain wheat noodles from Japan. They are available fresh, pre-cooked or dried.

cellophane noodles

egg noodles

rice noodles

soba noodles

somen noodles

udon noodles

Noodle Know-how

- *Store dried noodles in airtight boxes and store fresh noodles in the refrigerator, having checked the use-by date on the packaging.*
- *As a general rule, allow 75–115g/3–4oz noodles per person.*
- *Many recipes call for noodles to be soaked in warm water before being cooked; check the recipe, as you need to allow the requisite time.*
- *It is easy to overcook noodles. Remove them from the heat when they are barely tender and drain them in a colander. If you are not using them immediately, rinse them under cold running water so they stop cooking, then drain them again.*
- *If you are going to fry the prepared noodles, it is a good idea to blot them dry with kitchen paper.*

Basic Pasta Dough

Making pasta dough at home isn't difficult, especially if you use a food processor and a pasta machine. If you have neither, make the pasta by hand. It may not end up quite so thin as you would like, but it will still taste delicious. For enough pasta to serve 3–4 people, you will need 200g/7oz/1¾ cups plain (all-purpose) white flour, a pinch of salt, 2 eggs and 15ml/1 tbsp olive oil. You can also use strong white bread flour. If you are going to make flavoured pasta (see below), the quantities may need to be slightly changed.

To make the dough by hand

1 To make the dough by hand, sift the flour and salt into a heap on a clean work surface and make a well in the centre with your fist.

2 Lightly beat the eggs with the oil and pour into the well. Mix the egg mixture into the flour with your fingers. Alternatively, add the eggs and oil to the well and beat lightly with a fork, gradually drawing in the flour.

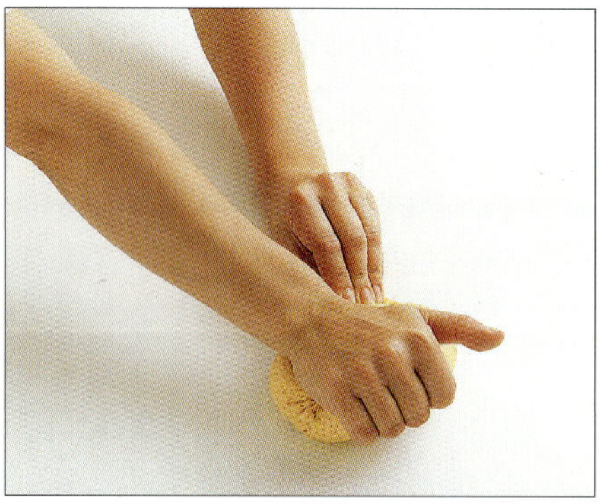

3 Knead the pasta until smooth, wrap it and set it aside to rest for at least 30 minutes before rolling it out. It will be much more elastic after resting.

To make the dough in a food processor

1 Sift the flour into the bowl of a food processor and add the salt.

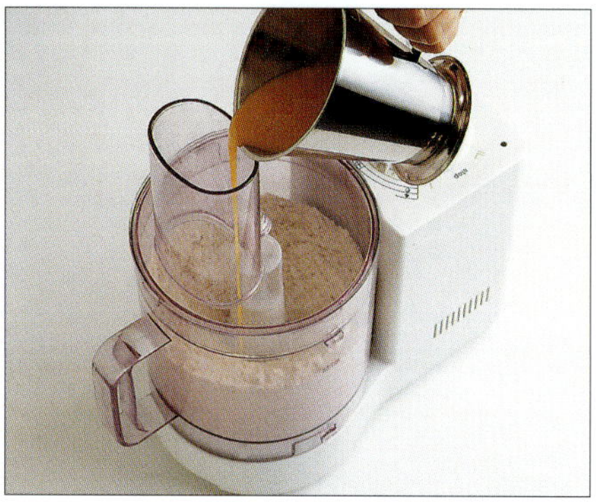

2 Lightly beat the eggs with the oil and pour them in, together with any chosen flavouring. Process until the dough begins to come together, then tip it out and knead it until smooth. Wrap and rest for 40 minutes before shaping.

Variations

Tomato Pasta *Add 30ml/2 tbsp tomato purée (paste) to the flour and use only 1½ eggs.*

Herb Pasta *Add 45ml/3 tbsp chopped fresh herbs to the flour.*

Wholemeal Pasta *Use 150g/5oz/1¼ cups wholemeal (whole-wheat) flour sifted with 25g/1oz/¼ cup plain (all-purpose) white flour.*

Spinach Pasta *Cook 150g/5oz frozen leaf spinach, squeeze out the moisture, then blend with 2 eggs. Use a little extra flour if the dough is sticky.*

To shape the dough in a pasta machine

1 Feed it several times through the machine, using the highest setting first, then reducing the setting until the required thickness is achieved.

2 Fit the special cutter and turn the handle if you want to produce fettuccine or tagliatelle. A narrower cutter will produce spaghetti or tagliarini. Toss the pasta lightly in flour and spread it out on floured dishtowels to dry.

Cook's Tip

The quantities given are guidelines, rather than hard-and-fast rules. Both the humidity on the day that you are making pasta and the type of flour you are using will affect the texture. The dough should not be too soft – it should be quite hard to knead – so extra flour may be required. However, too much extra will make the pasta tough and taste floury. With practice, you will get to know the "feel".

Shaping Pasta by Hand

Making your own noodles and pasta shapes is immensely satisfying and not as difficult as you might expect. Who cares if the results are not perfectly uniform? Being able to shape your own tagliatelle, ravioli and tortellini is great fun. In the case of filled shapes, it means you can experiment with different fillings and alter the size or shape. Guidance is given here for cutting or shaping three basic styles of pasta, and you will find more suggestions among the recipes in the book. Be bold – you'll be designing your own pasta in no time.

Ravioli

1 To make ravioli, use half the dough at a time, keeping the rest wrapped in clear film (plastic wrap). On a lightly floured surface, roll out one piece of pasta thinly to a neat rectangle. Cover with a damp, clean dishtowel and roll out an identical rectangle from the remaining pasta. Pipe or spoon small mounds of filling on to one sheet of pasta, spacing them at 4cm/1½in intervals. Brush the spaces in between with beaten egg or water.

2 Gently lay the remaining pasta rectangle over the topped dough. Press down firmly between the pockets of filling, pushing out any air.

3 Cut the dough into squares, using a serrated ravioli cutter or a sharp knife. Spread out the ravioli on floured dishtowels and leave to dry for about 30 minutes before cooking.

Tortellini

1 To make tortellini, stamp out thin rounds of pasta, using a round ravioli or biscuit (cookie) cutter. Pipe or spoon the filling into the middle, then brush the edges with beaten egg or water.

2 Fold each round into a crescent, excluding all the air. Bend the two edges round to meet each other and press them together to seal. When all the tortellini have been shaped, spread them on floured dishtowels and leave to dry for 30 minutes before cooking.

Tagliatelle

1 To make tagliatelle, lightly flour a thin sheet of pasta dough, then roll it up in the same way as a Swiss (jelly) roll.

2 Cut the roll into thin slices, using a sharp knife. Immediately unravel the slices to uncurl the pasta ribbons, which should then be lightly tossed in flour and spread on floured dishtowels to dry. (To make tagliarini, cut the rolled-up dough into slices 3mm/⅛in thick. To make pappardelle, simply roll out the dough and cut it into wide ribbons.)

Cooking Pasta

Allow 75–175g/3–6oz of pasta per person, depending on whether the pasta is for an appetizer or main course and bearing in mind the accompanying sauce.

Bring a large pan of lightly salted water to the boil. For long shapes, such as spaghetti, hold all the pasta in one hand and gradually lower it into the water until it softens sufficiently to curl round into the pan and eventually becomes immersed completely. Sprinkle shapes into the pan, trying not to let the water go off the boil.

Cooking times vary but, on average, fresh, unfilled pasta takes 2–3 minutes, although very fine pasta may cook almost instantly. Fresh filled pasta requires 8–10 minutes. Dried unfilled pasta needs to boil for 8–12 minutes and dried filled pasta requires about 15–20 minutes. Always test by tasting – the pasta should be *al dente*; tender, but firm enough to retain a bit of "bite".

SOUPS & SALADS

There are few things more appetizing and delicious than home-made soup and adding little pasta shapes or Asian noodles turns it into a really satisfying and substantial dish. Just serve with a chunk of fresh bread for a warming and filling lunch on even the coldest day. This chapter features hearty, traditional soups, such as Fresh Pea & Ham, delicately flavoured appetizers, such as Consommé with Agnolotti, and exotic Asian classics, such as Seafood Laksa. All are really quite easy to prepare and some are surprisingly quick, too. Pasta salads are always popular – not least because they look so attractive. Served warm or cold, pasta combines superbly with a vast range of salad ingredients, from vegetables to fish and from chicken to cheese. They are the ideal choice for summer entertaining, as they can be prepared in advance, but still retain their refreshing "bite". This fabulous collection of recipes includes easy salads that can be assembled in moments from the store cupboard, sophisticated combinations of luxurious ingredients for the perfect dinner-party appetizer, Mediterranean medleys for a lingering *al fresco* lunch and piquant noodle dishes to liven up the taste buds. For a salad that is just a little different, whether to brighten up a midweek family supper, entertain unexpected visitors or to intrigue and impress guests, look no further – a pasta salad will fit the bill.

Consommé with Agnolotti

A clear winner, this delectable soup features round pasta shapes with a shellfish filling.

Serves 4–6
75g/3oz/¾ cup cooked peeled prawns (shrimp)
75g/3oz canned crab meat, drained
5ml/1 tsp finely grated fresh root ginger
15ml/1 tbsp fresh white breadcrumbs
5ml/1 tsp light soy sauce
1 spring onion (scallion), finely chopped
1 garlic clove, crushed
1 quantity Basic Pasta Dough
1 egg white, beaten
400g/14oz can chicken consommé
30ml/2 tbsp sherry
salt and freshly ground black pepper
50g/2oz/1/2 cup peeled cooked prawns (shrimp) and fresh coriander (cilantro) leaves, to garnish

1 Put the prawns, crab meat, ginger, breadcrumbs, soy sauce, onion and garlic into a food processor or blender. Season well, then process until smooth.

2 Roll the pasta into thin sheets. Stamp out 32 rounds, each 5cm/2in in diameter, with a fluted pastry cutter.

3 Place a small teaspoon of the filling in the centre of half the pasta rounds. Brush the edges of each round with egg white and sandwich with a second round on top. Pinch the edges together firmly to stop the filling from seeping out.

4 Cook the pasta, in batches, in a large pan of boiling, salted water until *al dente*. As each round cooks, lift it out and drop it into a bowl of cold water. Leave for 5 seconds before draining and placing on a tray.

5 Heat the consommé in a pan with the sherry. When piping hot, add the cooked pasta shapes and simmer for 1–2 minutes, until just heated through. Serve the agnolotti in warmed, shallow soup bowls, covered with hot consommé. Garnish with extra peeled prawns and fresh coriander leaves.

Provençal Fish Soup with Pasta

This stunning soup has all the flavours of the Mediterranean. Serve it as a main course for a deliciously filling lunch.

Serves 4
30ml/2 tbsp olive oil
1 onion, sliced
1 garlic clove, crushed
1 leek, sliced
1 litre/1¾ pints/4 cups water
225g/8oz canned chopped tomatoes
5ml/1 tsp dried oregano
1.5ml/¼ tsp saffron threads (optional)
115g/4oz/1 cup small dried pasta shapes
450g/1lb skinned white fish fillets, cut into bitesize chunks
about 8 tightly closed live mussels, scrubbed and bearded
salt and freshly ground black pepper
sliced French bread, to serve

For the rouille
2 garlic cloves, crushed
1 drained canned pimiento, chopped
15ml/1 tbsp fresh white breadcrumbs
60ml/4 tbsp mayonnaise

1 First, make the rouille by pounding the garlic, canned pimiento and breadcrumbs together in mortar with a pestle (or in a food processor). Stir in the mayonnaise and season to taste with salt and pepper. Set aside.

2 Heat the olive oil in a large pan and add the onion, garlic and leek. Cover and cook gently, stirring occasionally, for 5 minutes, until soft.

3 Pour in the water, then add the chopped tomatoes, oregano and saffron threads, if using. Season with salt and pepper and cook for 15–20 minutes.

4 Add the pasta shapes and cook for 5 minutes, then add the fish and place the mussels on top. Simmer with the lid on for 5–10 minutes, until the mussels open and the fish is just cooked. (If any mussels fail to open, discard them.)

5 Toast the French bread, spread it with the rouille and serve immediately with the soup.

Chickpea Soup with Ditalini

Chickpeas are often neglected when it comes to choosing ingredients for soup, but really prove their worth in this classic recipe from central Italy.

Serves 4–6

200g/7oz/1 cup dried chickpeas, soaked overnight in water to cover
3 garlic cloves, peeled but left whole
1 bay leaf
90ml/6 tbsp olive oil
50g/2oz/ ¼ cup diced salt pork, pancetta or bacon
1 fresh rosemary sprig, plus extra to garnish
600ml/1 pint/2½ cups water
150g/5oz/1¼ cups dried ditalini or other short hollow pasta shapes
salt and freshly ground black pepper
freshly grated Parmesan cheese, to serve

1 Drain the chickpeas, rinse them under cold water and drain them again. Put them in a large pan with fresh water to cover. Boil for 15 minutes. Rinse and drain.

2 Return the chickpeas to the pan and again pour in water to cover. Add one garlic clove, the bay leaf and 45ml/3 tbsp of the oil and season with a pinch of pepper.

3 Bring to the boil, then lower the heat and simmer for about 2 hours, or until tender, adding more water as necessary. Remove the bay leaf. Lift out half the chickpeas with a slotted spoon and process them in a food processor with a few tablespoons of the cooking liquid. Return the purée to the pan.

4 In a frying pan, sauté the diced pork, pancetta or bacon gently in the remaining oil with the rosemary and remaining whole garlic cloves until just golden. Discard the rosemary and garlic.

5 Stir the pork with its oils into the chickpea mixture, then add the water and bring to the boil. Adjust the seasoning, if necessary. Stir in the pasta and cook until *al dente*. Serve in warmed bowls garnished with rosemary. Pass the grated Parmesan cheese separately.

Fresh Pea & Ham Soup

Frozen peas provide flavour, freshness and colour in this delicious winter soup, which is filling enough to make a light main course.

Serves 4

115g/4oz/1 cup small pasta shapes
30ml/2 tbsp vegetable oil
1 small bunch spring onions (scallions), chopped
350g/12oz/3 cups frozen peas
1.2 litres/2 pints/5 cups chicken stock
225g/8oz raw unsmoked ham or gammon (cured ham)
60ml/4 tbsp double (heavy) cream
salt and freshly ground black pepper
warm crusty bread, to serve

1 Bring a large pan of salted water to the boil. Toss in the pasta and cook until it is *al dente*. Drain, cover with cold water and set aside until required.

2 Heat the vegetable oil in a large, heavy pan, then add the spring onions and cook, stirring occasionally, until soft. Add the peas and chicken stock. Bring to the boil, then lower the heat and simmer for 10 minutes.

3 Leave the mixture to cool slightly. Process in a blender or food processor, then pour the purée back into the pan. Heat to simmering point.

4 Cut the ham or gammon into short fingers and add it to the pan. Drain and add the pasta. Simmer for 2–3 minutes, then season to taste with salt and pepper. Stir in the cream and serve with the warm crusty bread.

Variation
Any pasta shapes can be used for this soup, although hoops or shells seem to work best of all. Whatever shape you choose, make sure that the pasta is not larger than the other ingredients in the soup.

Courgette Soup with Pastina

Perfect for a summer lunch, this pretty green soup is light and fresh-tasting.

Serves 4–6

60ml/4 tbsp olive or sunflower oil
2 onions, finely chopped
1.5 litres/2½ pints/6 cups chicken stock
900g/2lb courgettes (zucchini), grated
115g/4oz/1 cup pastina (small soup pasta shapes)
fresh lemon juice
30ml/2 tbsp chopped fresh chervil
salt and freshly ground black pepper
sour cream, to serve

1 Heat the oil in a large pan and add the onions. Cover and cook gently for about 20 minutes, until very soft but not coloured, stirring occasionally.

2 Add the stock. Bring to the boil, then stir in the courgettes and pasta. Simmer until the pasta is *al dente*.

3 Season to taste with lemon juice, salt and pepper. Stir in the chervil. Serve in warmed bowls, adding a swirl of sour cream.

Variations
Cucumber can be used instead of courgettes (zucchini). If you don't have any fresh stock, use canned chicken consommé.

Pumpkin & Spaghetti Soup

Creamy and rich, pumpkin soup is a wonderful way to celebrate the time of harvest and tastes especially good when spaghetti and Parmesan are added.

Serves 4

50g/2oz/¼ cup butter
1 onion, finely chopped
450g/1lb piece of peeled pumpkin, cubed
750ml/1¼ pints/3 cups chicken or vegetable stock
475ml/16fl oz/2 cups milk
pinch of freshly grated nutmeg
40g/1½ oz dried spaghetti, broken into short lengths
90ml/6 tbsp freshly grated Parmesan cheese
salt and freshly ground black pepper

1 Heat the butter in a heavy pan and fry the onion over a low heat for 8 minutes. Stir in the pumpkin and cook for about 2–3 minutes more.
2 Pour in the stock, bring to the boil, then lower the heat and cook for about 15 minutes, or until the pumpkin is soft.
3 Remove from the heat and leave the mixture to cool slightly. Transfer it to a blender or food processor, process to a purée, then scrape it back into the pan. Stir in the milk and nutmeg, with salt and pepper to taste. Bring to the boil.
4 Add the spaghetti and cook until it is *al dente*. Stir in the Parmesan and serve immediately.

Little Stuffed Hats in Broth

Cappelletti – little hats – are so delicious that you do not need an elaborate soup in which to serve them. Chicken stock, a splash of white wine and fresh herbs are all that are needed.

Serves 4

1.2 litres/2 pints/5 cups chicken stock
90–115g/3½–4oz/1 cup fresh or dried cappelletti
30ml/2 tbsp dry white wine
about 15ml/1 tbsp finely chopped fresh flat leaf parsley
salt and freshly ground black pepper
shredded flat leaf parsley, to garnish
about 30ml/2 tbsp freshly grated Parmesan cheese, to serve

1 Pour the chicken stock into a large pan and bring it to the boil. Season to taste, then add the pasta. When the stock boils, lower the heat and simmer, stirring frequently, until the pasta is *al dente*.

2 Swirl in the wine and chopped parsley, then taste for seasoning. Ladle into four warmed soup plates. Garnish with shredded flat leaf parsley, sprinkle with grated Parmesan cheese and serve immediately.

Cook's Tip
Cappelletti are very similar in shape to tortellini. You can buy them from delicatessens and supermarkets or make your own, and you can use either fresh or dried pasta.

Minestrone

This soup crops up on restaurant menus the world over, but seldom tastes as good as when made in a country kitchen from freshly picked vegetables.

Serves 6–8

30ml/2 tbsp olive oil
50g/2oz rindless smoked streaky (fatty) bacon rashers (strips), diced
2 large onions, sliced
2 garlic cloves, crushed
2 carrots, diced
3 celery sticks, sliced
225g/8oz/generous 1 cup dried haricot (navy) beans, soaked overnight in water to cover
400g/14oz can chopped tomatoes
2.5 litres/4 pints/10 cups beef stock
3 potatoes, peeled and diced
175g/6oz/1½ cups small pasta shapes
225g/8oz green cabbage, thinly sliced
175g/6oz fine green beans, sliced
115g/4oz/1 cup frozen peas
45ml/3 tbsp chopped fresh parsley
salt and freshly ground black pepper
freshly grated Parmesan cheese, to serve

1 Heat the oil in a large pan and gently fry the bacon, onions and garlic, stirring occasionally, for 5 minutes, until soft.

2 Add the carrots and celery and cook for 2–3 minutes, then drain the beans and add them to the pan with the tomatoes and stock. Bring to the boil, lower the heat, cover and simmer for 2 hours, or until the haricot beans are almost tender.

3 Add the potatoes and cook for 15 minutes more, then add the pasta, cabbage, green beans and peas. Cook for 15 minutes, until the pasta is *al dente*. Season to taste, stir in the parsley and serve with Parmesan cheese.

Variation

For a delicious change, borrowed from Genoese cooks, stir in a little pesto just before serving.

Rich Minestrone

This is a special minestrone made with chicken. Served with crusty Italian bread, it makes a hearty meal.

Serves 4–6

15ml/1 tbsp olive oil
2 chicken thighs
3 rindless streaky (fatty) bacon rashers (strips), chopped
1 onion, finely chopped
a few fresh basil leaves, shredded
a few fresh rosemary leaves, finely chopped
15ml/1 tbsp chopped fresh flat leaf parsley
2 potatoes, peeled and cut into 1cm/½in cubes
1 large carrot, cut into 1cm/½in cubes
2 small courgettes (zucchini), cut into 1cm/½in cubes
1–2 celery sticks, cut into 1cm/½in cubes
1 litre/1¾ pints/4 cups chicken stock
200g/7oz/1¾ cups frozen peas
90g/3½ oz/scant 1 cup dried stellette or other soup pasta
salt and freshly ground black pepper
fresh basil leaves, to garnish
coarsely shaved Parmesan cheese, to serve

1 Heat the oil in a large frying pan and fry the chicken thighs for about 5 minutes on each side. Remove with a slotted spoon and set aside.

2 Add the bacon, onion and herbs to the pan and cook gently, stirring constantly, for 5 minutes. Add the remaining vegetables, except the peas, and cook for 5–7 minutes, stirring frequently. Return the chicken thighs to the pan, add the stock and bring to the boil. Cover and cook over a low heat for 35–40 minutes, stirring occasionally.

3 Remove the chicken with a slotted spoon and place on a board. Stir the peas and pasta into the soup, bring back to the boil and simmer, stirring frequently, until the pasta is *al dente*.

4 Remove the chicken skin, cut the meat from the bones into 1cm/½in pieces. Return the meat to the soup and heat. Taste for seasoning. Serve in warmed soup bowls. Garnish with one to two basil leaves and sprinkle over Parmesan shavings.

Seafood Laksa

The red chillies in the paste make this a very spicy soup.

Serves 4

4 fresh red chillies, seeded and roughly chopped
1 onion, roughly chopped
1cm/ ½in cube shrimp paste
1 lemon grass stalk, chopped
1 small piece of fresh root ginger, roughly chopped
6 macadamia nuts
60ml/4 tbsp vegetable oil
5ml/1 tsp paprika
5ml/1 tsp ground turmeric
475ml/16fl oz/2 cups fish stock or water
600ml/1 pint/2½ cups canned coconut milk
dash of fish sauce
12 raw king prawns (jumbo shrimp), peeled and deveined
8 scallops, shelled
225g/8oz prepared squid, cut into rings
350g/12oz rice vermicelli, soaked in warm water until soft
salt and freshly ground black pepper
lime halves, to serve

For the garnish

¼ cucumber, cut into thin batons
2 fresh red chillies, seeded and thinly sliced
30ml/2 tbsp fresh mint leaves
30ml/2 tbsp fried shallots or onions

1 In a blender or food processor, process the chillies, onion, shrimp paste, lemon grass, ginger and nuts until smooth.

2 Heat 45ml/3 tbsp of the oil in a large pan. Add the chilli paste and fry for 6 minutes. Stir in the paprika and turmeric and fry for 2 minutes more.

3 Pour in the stock or water and the coconut milk. Bring to the boil, lower the heat and simmer gently for 15–20 minutes. Season to taste with the fish sauce.

4 Season the seafood with salt and pepper. Heat the remaining oil in a frying pan and fry the seafood for 2–3 minutes.

5 Add the noodles to the soup and heat through. Divide among warmed serving bowls. Place the fried shellfish on top, then garnish with the cucumber, chillies, mint and fried shallots or onions. Serve with the lime halves.

Chicken Soup with Noodles

Warm spices, such as paprika and cinnamon, give this chicken soup a superb flavour.

Serves 4–6

30ml/2 tbsp sunflower oil
15g/ ½oz/1 tbsp butter
1 onion, chopped
2 chicken legs quartered
2 carrots, cut into 4cm/ 1½in pieces
1 parsnip, cut into 4cm/ 1½in pieces
1.5 litres/2½ pints/6 cups chicken stock
1 cinnamon stick
good pinch of paprika
2 egg yolks
juice of ½ lemon
30ml/2 tbsp chopped fresh coriander (cilantro)
30ml/2 tbsp chopped fresh parsley
pinch of saffron threads, soaked for 10 minutes in 30ml/2 tbsp boiling water
150g/5oz egg noodles
salt and freshly ground black pepper

1 Heat the oil and butter in a large pan and fry the onion until softened. Add the chicken pieces and fry them with the onion until brown on all sides.

2 Transfer the chicken to a plate and add the carrot and parsnip pieces to the pan. Cook over a low heat, stirring frequently, for 3–4 minutes, then return the chicken to the pan. Stir in the stock, cinnamon stick and paprika. Season well. Bring to the boil, lower the heat, cover and simmer for 1 hour, until the vegetables are very tender.

3 Beat the egg yolks with the lemon juice in a bowl. Add the chopped coriander and parsley, then stir in the saffron water.

4 Lift the chicken pieces out of the soup and put them on a plate. Spoon off any fat from the soup, then increase the heat and stir in the noodles. Cook until the noodles are *al dente*.

5 Meanwhile, skin the chicken and chop the flesh into bitesize pieces. Add to the soup, with the egg mixture. Cook over a very low heat for 1–2 minutes, stirring constantly. Adjust the seasoning and serve immediately.

Chiang Mai Noodle Soup

A signature dish of the Thai city of Chiang Mai, this is a delicious soup.

Serves 4–6

600ml/1 pint/2½ cups canned coconut milk
30ml/2 tbsp bottled red curry paste
5ml/1 tsp ground turmeric
450g/1lb skinless, boneless chicken thighs, cut into bitesize chunks
600ml/1 pint/2½ cups chicken stock
60ml/4 tbsp fish sauce
15ml/1 tbsp dark soy sauce
juice of 1 lime
450g/1lb fresh egg noodles, blanched briefly in boiling water

For the garnish

3 spring onions (scallions), chopped
4 fresh red chillies, chopped
4 shallots, chopped
60ml/4 tbsp sliced pickled mustard leaves, rinsed
30ml/2 tbsp fried sliced garlic
fresh coriander (cilantro) leaves

1 Pour one-third of the coconut milk into a large pan. Bring to the boil, stirring with a wooden spoon, until it separates.

2 Stir in the curry paste and ground turmeric and cook until fragrant, then add the chicken. Stir-fry for about 2 minutes, ensuring that all the chunks are coated with the paste.

3 Stir in the remaining coconut milk, the chicken stock, fish sauce and soy sauce. Bring to the boil, then simmer gently for 7–10 minutes. Remove from the heat and stir in the lime juice.

4 Reheat the noodles in boiling water, drain and divide among warmed individual bowls. Divide the soup among the bowls, making sure that the chicken pieces are evenly distributed. Top each serving with a little of each of the garnishes.

Cook's Tip

The quantity of fish sauce suggested here will give the soup quite a pronounced flavour. If you are not sure you will like it, start by using less.

Chicken & Buckwheat Noodle Soup

Buckwheat or soba noodles, served in hot, deliciously seasoned broth, are very popular in Japan.

Serves 4

225g/8oz skinless, boneless chicken breast portions
120ml/4fl oz/½ cup soy sauce
15ml/1 tbsp sake
1 litres/1¾ pints/4 cups chicken stock
2 pieces of young leek, cut into 2.5cm/1in strips
175g/6oz spinach leaves, shredded
300g/11oz buckwheat or soba noodles
toasted sesame seeds, to garnish

1 Slice the chicken diagonally into bitesize pieces. Combine the soy sauce and sake in a pan. Bring to a simmer over a low heat. Add the chicken and cook gently for about 3 minutes, until it is tender. Keep hot.

2 Bring the stock to the boil in a separate pan. Add the leek strips and simmer for 3 minutes, then add the spinach. Remove from the heat, but keep hot.

3 Cook the noodles in a large pan of boiling water, following the instructions on the packet, until *al dente*.

4 Drain the noodles and divide them among warmed shallow bowls. Ladle the hot soup into the bowls, then add a portion of chicken to each. Serve, sprinkled with sesame seeds.

Cook's Tips

- *If you make your own chicken stock for this recipe, flavour it with 2 slices of fresh root ginger, 2 garlic cloves, 4 spring onions (scallions), 2 celery sticks, a handful of coriander (cilantro) stalks and a few crushed black peppercorns.*
- *For an authentic flavour, use Japanese soy sauce, which is not so strong as Chinese. Known as shoyu, it is available from specialist stores and some supermarkets. Best for clear broths, usukuchi soy sauce is light coloured and quite salty.*

Tuna Pasta Salad

This easy pasta salad uses canned beans and tuna for a quick main dish.

Serves 6–8

450g/1lb/4 cups dried short pasta, such as ruote, macaroni or farfalle
60ml/4 tbsp olive oil
2 x 200g/7oz cans tuna in oil, drained
2 x 400g/14oz cans cannellini or borlotti beans, rinsed and drained
1 small red onion
2 celery sticks
juice of 1 lemon
30ml/2 tbsp chopped fresh parsley
salt and freshly ground black pepper
fresh parsley, to garnish

1 Bring a large pan of lightly salted water to the boil and cook the pasta until it is *al dente*. Drain, rinse under cold water, drain again and tip into a bowl. Add the oil and toss well. Set aside until cold.

2 Flake the tuna and add it to the cooked pasta with the beans. Toss lightly. Slice the onion and celery very thinly, add them to the pasta mixture and toss again.

3 Mix the lemon juice and parsley in a bowl, then add the mixture to the salad. Season with salt and pepper to taste. Mix thoroughly. Leave the salad to stand for at least 1 hour before serving at room temperature, garnished with parsley.

Variations

- *Use smoked fish, such as mackerel or trout, instead of the canned tuna.*
- *Substitute canned or fresh crab meat for the tuna and 15ml/1 tbsp chopped fresh dill for the parsley.*
- *Replace 1 can of beans with 275g/10oz lightly steamed mangetouts (snow peas) or sugar snap peas.*

Mediterranean Salad with Basil

A type of Salade Niçoise with pasta, this conjures up all the sunny flavours of the Mediterranean.

Serves 4

175g/6oz fine green beans, trimmed
225g/8oz/2 cups chunky dried pasta shapes
2 large ripe tomatoes
50g/2oz/2 cups fresh basil leaves
200g/7oz can tuna in oil, drained
2 hard-boiled (hard-cooked) eggs, sliced or quartered
50g/2oz can anchovy fillets, drained
drained capers and pitted black olives, to garnish

For the dressing

90ml/6 tbsp extra virgin olive oil
30ml/2 tbsp white wine vinegar or lemon juice
2 garlic cloves, crushed
2.5ml/½ tsp Dijon mustard
30ml/2 tbsp chopped fresh basil
salt and freshly ground black pepper

1 Whisk all the ingredients for the dressing together and leave to infuse (steep) while you make the salad.

2 Bring a large pan of water to the boil. Add the beans and blanch for 2–3 minutes. Using a slotted spoon, transfer them to a colander. Refresh under cold water, drain well and set aside.

3 Bring the pan of water back to the boil and cook the pasta until it is *al dente*. Drain, rinse under cold water and drain again. Put in a bowl and toss with a little of the dressing.

4 Slice or quarter the tomatoes and arrange them on the bottom of a bowl. Moisten them with a little dressing and cover with one-quarter of the basil leaves. Then cover with the beans. Moisten with a little more dressing and cover with one-third of the remaining basil.

5 Cover with the dressed pasta and half the remaining basil. Roughly flake the tuna and add it to the salad. Arrange the eggs on top, then finally sprinkle over the anchovy fillets, capers and black olives. Pour over the remaining dressing and garnish with the remaining basil. Serve immediately.

Warm Scallop & Conchiglie Salad

This is a very special modern dish, a warm salad composed of scallops, pasta and fresh rocket flavoured with roasted pepper, chilli and balsamic vinegar.

Serves 4

8 large fresh scallops
300g/11oz/2¾ cups dried conchiglie
15ml/1 tbsp olive oil
15g/½oz/1 tbsp butter
120ml/4fl oz/ ½ cup dry white wine
90g/3½ oz rocket (arugula) leaves, stalks trimmed
salt and freshly ground black pepper

For the vinaigrette

60ml/4 tbsp extra virgin olive oil
15ml/1 tbsp balsamic vinegar
1 piece bottled roasted (bell) pepper, drained and finely chopped
1–2 fresh red chillies, seeded and chopped
1 garlic clove, crushed
5–10ml/1–2 tbsp clear honey, to taste

1 Cut each scallop into two to three pieces. If the corals are attached, pull them off and cut each piece in half. Season the scallops and corals with salt and pepper.

2 Make the vinaigrette. Put the oil, vinegar, pepper and chillies in a jug (pitcher). Add the garlic and honey, and whisk well.

3 Bring a large pan of lightly salted water to the boil and cook the pasta until it is *al dente*.

4 Meanwhile, heat the oil and butter in a non-stick frying pan until sizzling. Add half the scallops and toss over a high heat for 2 minutes. Remove with a slotted spoon and keep warm. Cook the remaining scallops in the same way.

5 Add the wine to the liquid remaining in the pan and stir over a high heat until the mixture has reduced to a few tablespoons. Remove from the heat and keep warm. Drain the pasta and tip it into a warmed bowl. Add the rocket, scallops, the reduced cooking juices and the vinaigrette and toss well to combine. Serve immediately.

Smoked Salmon & Dill Pasta Salad

This dish makes a main course for two or appetizer for four.

Serves 2–4

350g/12oz/3 cups dried fusilli
6 large fresh dill sprigs, chopped, plus extra sprigs to garnish
30ml/2 tbsp extra virgin olive oil
15ml/1 tbsp white wine vinegar
300ml/½ pint/1¼ cups double (heavy) cream
175g/6oz smoked salmon
salt and freshly ground black pepper

1 Bring a large pan of lightly salted water to the boil and cook the pasta until it is *al dente*. Drain, rinse under cold water, drain again and tip into a bowl. Set aside until cold.

2 Make the dressing. Place the chopped dill, olive oil, vinegar and cream in a food processor and process until smooth. Season to taste with salt and pepper.

3 Slice the salmon into small strips. Place the cooled pasta and the smoked salmon in a large mixing bowl. Pour on the dressing and toss carefully. Transfer to a serving bowl, garnish with the extra dill sprigs and serve immediately.

Warm Smoked Salmon & Pasta Salad

This is an elegant salad.

Serves 4

350g/12oz dried spaghetti
15ml/1 tbsp extra virgin olive oil
1 garlic clove, crushed
75g/3oz smoked salmon, cut into thin strips
1 bunch of watercress, leaves removed and stems discarded
salt and freshly ground black pepper

1 Bring a large pan of lightly salted water to the boil and cook the pasta until it is *al dente*. Drain and toss in half the oil.
2 Heat the remaining oil in a heavy frying pan and stir-fry the garlic for 30 seconds. Add the salmon and watercress, season with pepper and stir-fry for 30 seconds.
3 Spoon the mixture on to the pasta, toss and serve warm.

Pink & Green Salad

Spiked with a little fresh chilli, this pretty salad makes a delicious light lunch when served with hot fresh ciabatta rolls.

Serves 4

225g/8oz/2 cups dried farfalle
juice of ½ lemon
1 small fresh red chilli, seeded and very finely chopped
60ml/4 tbsp chopped fresh basil
30ml/2 tbsp chopped fresh coriander (cilantro)
60ml/4 tbsp extra virgin olive oil
15ml/1 tbsp mayonnaise
250g/9oz/2¼ cups cooked peeled prawns (shrimp)
1 avocado
salt and freshly ground black pepper

1 Bring a large pan of lightly salted water to the boil and cook the pasta until it is *al dente*. Drain, rinse under cold water and drain again. Leave until cold.

2 Put the lemon juice and chilli in a bowl with half the basil and coriander and season with salt and pepper to taste. Whisk well to mix, then gradually add the oil and mayonnaise, whisking until the dressing is thick.

3 Add the prawns to the dressing and stir gently until they are evenly coated.

4 Cut the avocado in half, lift out the stone (pit) and remove the peel. Cut the flesh into neat dice. Add the avocado to the prawns and dressing with the pasta, toss well to mix and taste for seasoning. Serve immediately, sprinkled with the remaining basil and coriander.

Cook's Tip
This pasta salad can be made several hours ahead of time, but without adding the avocado. Cover the bowl with clear film (plastic wrap) and chill it in the refrigerator until required. Prepare the avocado and add it to the salad just before serving or it will discolour, turning brown, and spoil the effect.

Seafood Salad

This is a very special salad which would look quite spectacular with one of the new and unusual "designer" shapes of pasta.

Serves 4–6

450g/1lb live mussels, scrubbed and bearded
250ml/8fl oz/1 cup dry white wine
2 garlic cloves, roughly chopped
a handful of fresh flat leaf parsley
175g/6oz prepared squid rings
175g/6oz/1½ cups small dried pasta shapes
175g/6oz/1½ cups cooked peeled prawns (shrimp)

For the dressing
90ml/6 tbsp extra virgin olive oil
juice of 1 lemon
5–10ml/1–2 tsp drained capers, roughly chopped
1 garlic clove, crushed
a small handful of fresh flat leaf parsley, finely chopped
salt and freshly ground black pepper

1 Check over the mussels and discard any that are damaged, open or that do not close when sharply tapped with the back of a knife.

2 Pour half the wine into a large pan and add the garlic, parsley and mussels. Cover the pan tightly and bring to the boil over a high heat. Cook for about 5 minutes, shaking the pan frequently, until the mussels have opened.

3 Tip the mussels and their liquid into a colander set over a bowl. Reserve a few mussels in their shells for garnishing, then remove the remainder from their shells, tipping the liquid from the mussels into the bowl of cooking liquid. Discard any mussels that remain closed.

4 Strain the mussel cooking liquid through a sieve lined with muslin (cheesecloth) and return it to the pan. Add the remaining wine and the squid rings. Bring to the boil, cover and simmer gently, stirring occasionally, for 30 minutes or until the squid is tender. Leave the squid to cool in the cooking liquid.

5 Meanwhile, bring a large pan of lightly salted water to the boil and cook the pasta until it is *al dente*.

6 Make the dressing. Put the oil, lemon juice, capers, garlic and parsley into a large bowl and whisk to combine. Season to taste with salt and pepper.

7 Drain the cooked pasta well, add it to the bowl of dressing and toss well to mix. Leave to cool.

8 Tip the cooled squid into a sieve and drain well, then rinse it lightly under cold water. Add the squid, shelled mussels and prawns to the dressed pasta and toss well to mix.

9 Cover the bowl tightly with clear film (plastic wrap) and chill in the refrigerator for about 4 hours. Toss well before serving, then garnish with the reserved mussels in their shells.

Pasta Salad with Salami & Olives

Garlic and herb dressing gives a Mediterranean flavour to a handful of ingredients from the kitchen stores and refrigerator, making this an excellent salad for serving in winter.

Serves 4

225g/8oz/2 cups dried gnocchi or conchiglie
50g/2oz/ ½ cup pitted black olives, quartered lengthways
75g/3oz thinly sliced salami, any skin removed, diced
½ small red onion, finely chopped
a large handful of fresh basil leaves

For the dressing

60ml/4 tbsp extra virgin olive oil
good pinch of granulated sugar
juice of ½ lemon
5ml/1 tsp Dijon mustard
10ml/2 tsp dried oregano
1 garlic clove, crushed
salt and freshly ground black pepper

1 Bring a large pan of lightly salted water to the boil and cook the pasta until it is *al dente*.

2 Meanwhile, make the dressing. Put the oil, sugar, lemon juice, mustard, oregano and garlic in a large bowl, season with a little salt and pepper to taste and whisk well to mix.

3 Drain the pasta thoroughly, add it to the bowl of dressing and toss thoroughly to mix. Leave the dressed pasta to cool, stirring occasionally.

4 When the pasta is cold, add the olives, salami, onion and basil and toss well to mix again. Taste and adjust the seasoning, if necessary, then serve.

Cook's Tip

There are many different types of Italian salami that can be used. Salame napoletano is coarse cut and peppery, salame milanese is fine cut and mild in flavour, and salame di Felino is said to be the best in Italy.

Warm Pasta Salad with Ham

An unusual asparagus dressing tops the tagliatelle in this tasty salad.

Serves 4

450g/1lb asparagus
1 small potato
60ml/4 tbsp olive oil
15ml/1 tbsp lemon juice
10ml/2 tsp Dijon mustard
120ml/4fl oz/ ½ cup vegetable stock
450g/1lb dried tagliatelle
225g/8oz sliced cooked ham, 5mm/ ¼in thick, cut into fingers
2 eggs, hard-boiled (hard-cooked) and sliced
50g/2oz Parmesan cheese, shaved
salt and freshly ground black pepper

1 Bring a pan of lightly salted water to the boil. Snap off the tough woody part of each asparagus spear, then cut each spear in half. Add the thicker halves to the boiling water and cook for 6 minutes, then throw in the tips and cook for 6 minutes more. Drain, refresh under cold water, then drain again.

2 Meanwhile, put the potato into a small pan of lightly salted cold water, bring to the boil and cook for 10 minutes, until just tender. Drain and set aside.

3 Set aside about eight asparagus tips for garnishing. Put the rest of the asparagus in a food processor and chop it coarsely. Add the potato, olive oil, lemon juice, mustard and stock.

4 Bring a large pan of lightly salted water to the boil and cook the pasta until it is *al dente*. Drain, rinse under cold water and drain again. Return to the clean pan, add the asparagus dressing and toss well.

5 Divide the dressed pasta among four warmed plates. Top with the ham, hard-boiled eggs and asparagus tips. Serve with the Parmesan shavings.

Chicken & Broccoli Salad

Gorgonzola makes a wonderful tangy salad dressing that goes well with both chicken and broccoli.

Serves 4

175g/6oz/generous 1 cup broccoli florets, divided into small sprigs
225g/8oz/2 cups dried farfalle
2 large cooked chicken breast portions

For the dressing

90g/3½oz Gorgonzola cheese
15ml/1 tbsp white wine vinegar
60ml/4 tbsp extra virgin olive oil
2.5–5ml/ ½–1 tsp finely chopped fresh sage, plus extra sage sprigs to garnish
salt and freshly ground black pepper

1 Bring a large pan of lightly salted water to the boil and cook the broccoli florets for 3 minutes. Using a slotted spoon, transfer them to a colander. Rinse under cold water, then spread out on dishtowels to drain and dry.

2 Bring the water in the pan back to the boil and cook the pasta until it is *al dente*. Drain, rinse under cold water and drain again. Leave until cold.

3 Remove the skin from the cooked chicken breast portions and cut the meat into bitesize pieces.

4 Make the dressing. Put the cheese in a large bowl and mash with a fork, then whisk in the wine vinegar followed by the oil and sage. Season with salt and pepper to taste. Add the pasta, chicken and broccoli. Toss well, then season to taste and serve, garnished with extra sage.

Variations

- *If you find the flavour of Gorgonzola too strong, try a milder variety, such as dolcelatte.*
- *This salad also works well with cooked turkey breast portions*
- *Add four halved cherry tomatoes for additional colour.*
- *Use equal quantities of broccoli and cauliflower florets.*

Chicken Pasta Salad

This is a delicious and easy way of using up leftover cooked chicken.

Serves 4

225g/8oz/2 cups dried fusilli, preferably mixed colours
30ml/2 tbsp bottled pesto
15ml/1 tbsp olive oil
1 beefsteak tomato, peeled and diced
12 pitted black olives
225g/8oz cooked green beans, cut into short lengths
350g/12oz cooked chicken, diced
salt and freshly ground black pepper
fresh basil, to garnish

1 Bring a large pan of lightly salted water to the boil and cook the pasta until *al dente*. Drain, rinse under cold water and drain again. Put it into a bowl and stir in the pesto and olive oil.

2 Add the tomato, olives, beans and chicken. Season to taste. Toss to mix and transfer to a serving platter. Garnish and serve.

Chicken & Pepper Pasta Salad

A variation on chicken salad.

Serves 4

350g/12oz/3 cups dried short pasta, such as mezze rigatoni, penne or fusilli
45ml/3 tbsp olive oil
225g/8oz cooked chicken, cubed
4 spring onions (scallions), chopped
2 small red and yellow (bell) peppers, diced
50g/2oz/ ½ cup pitted green olives
45ml/3 tbsp mayonnaise
5ml/1 tsp Worcestershire sauce
15ml/1 tbsp wine vinegar
salt and freshly ground black pepper
a few fresh basil leaves, to garnish

1 Bring a large pan of lightly salted water to the boil and cook the pasta until it is *al dente*. Drain, tip into a bowl and add the olive oil. Toss well to mix, then leave until cold.
2 Add the chicken, spring onions, peppers and olives. Mix the mayonnaise, Worcestershire sauce, vinegar and seasoning, add to the salad and toss. Chill for 1 hour, then garnish and serve.

Summer Salad with Pasta

Ripe red tomatoes, mozzarella and olives make a good base for a fresh and tangy salad that is perfect for a light summer lunch.

Serves 4

350g/12oz/3 cups dried penne
3 ripe tomatoes, diced
150g/5oz packet mozzarella di bufala, drained and diced
10 pitted black olives, sliced
10 pitted green olives, sliced
1 spring onion (scallion), thinly sliced diagonally
a handful of fresh basil leaves

For the dressing

90ml/6 tbsp extra virgin olive oil
15ml/1 tbsp balsamic vinegar or lemon juice
salt and freshly ground black pepper

1 Bring a large pan of lightly salted water to the boil and cook the pasta until it is *al dente*. Drain, rinse under cold water and drain again.

2 Make the dressing. Whisk the olive oil and balsamic vinegar or lemon juice in a large bowl and season with a little salt and pepper to taste.

3 Add the pasta, tomatoes, mozzarella, olives and spring onion to the dressing and toss together well. Taste for seasoning before serving, sprinkled with the basil leaves.

Cook's Tip
Mozzarella di bufala, made from buffalo milk, has more flavour than the type made with cow's milk. It is available from most delicatessens and supermarkets.

Variations
Make the salad more substantial by adding other ingredients, such as sliced (bell) peppers, flaked tuna, canned anchovy fillets or diced ham.

Country Pasta Salad

Colourful, tasty and nutritious, this is the ideal pasta salad for a picnic.

Serves 6

300g/11oz/2¾ cups dried fusilli
150g/5oz green beans, cut into 5cm/2in lengths
1 potato, about 150g/5oz, diced
200g/7oz cherry tomatoes, halved
2 spring onions (scallions), finely chopped
90g/3½oz Parmesan cheese, diced or coarsely shaved
6–8 pitted black olives, cut into rings
15–30ml/1–2 tbsp drained bottled capers

For the dressing

90ml/6 tbsp extra virgin olive oil
15ml/1 tbsp balsamic vinegar
15ml/1 tbsp chopped fresh flat leaf parsley
salt and freshly ground black pepper

1 Bring a large pan of lightly salted water to the boil and cook the pasta until it is *al dente*. Drain, rinse under cold water, then drain again. Leave to cool.

2 Heat a pan of salted water and cook the beans and diced potato for 5–6 minutes, or until tender. Drain and leave to cool.

3 Make the dressing. Put all the ingredients in a large bowl with salt and pepper to taste and whisk well to mix.

4 Add the tomatoes, spring onions, Parmesan, olive rings and capers to the bowl, then the pasta, beans and potato. Toss well. Cover and leave to stand for about 30 minutes before serving.

Cook's Tips
• *Buy a piece of fresh Parmesan from the delicatessen. This is the less mature, softer type, which is sold as a table cheese, rather than the hard, mature Parmesan used for grating.*
• *Pasta for a salad should be as dry as possible when it is mixed with the dressing and other ingredients, so drain it very well and shake the colander several times while it is cooling.*

Prawn Noodle Salad with Fragrant Herbs

A refreshing seafood salad.

Serves 4

115g/4oz cellophane noodles, soaked in hot water until soft
16 cooked peeled prawns (shrimp)
1 small green (bell) pepper, seeded and cut into strips
½ cucumber, cut into strips
1 tomato, cut into strips
2 shallots, thinly sliced
salt and freshly ground black pepper
fresh coriander (cilantro), to garnish

For the dressing

15ml/1 tbsp rice vinegar
30ml/2 tbsp Thai fish sauce
30ml/2 tbsp fresh lime juice
2.5ml/ ½ tsp grated fresh root ginger
1 lemon grass stalk, finely chopped
1 fresh red chilli, seeded and thinly sliced
30ml/2 tbsp coarsely chopped mint
a few fresh tarragon sprigs, coarsely chopped
15ml/1 tbsp chopped chives

1 Make the dressing by combining all the ingredients in a small bowl and whisking well. Season with a pinch of salt.

2 Bring a large pan of lightly salted water to the boil. Drain the noodles, then plunge them into the water for 1–2 minutes, until just tender. Drain, rinse under cold water and drain again.

3 In a large bowl, combine the noodles with the prawns, green pepper, cucumber, tomato and shallots. Lightly season with salt and pepper, then toss with the dressing.

4 Pile the noodles on individual plates, extracting the prawns and arranging them on top. Garnish with a few coriander leaves and serve immediately.

Variation
Instead of prawns (shrimp), try squid, mussels or crab meat.

Egg Noodle Salad with Sesame Chicken

Dressed noodles with blanched vegetables make a delicious base for tender chicken slices.

Serves 4–6

400g/14oz fresh thin egg noodles
1 carrot, cut into long fine strips
50g/2oz/ ½ cup mangetouts (snow peas), cut into fine strips and blanched
115g/4oz/2 cups beansprouts, blanched
30ml/2 tbsp vegetable oil
225g/8oz skinless, boneless chicken breast portions, thinly sliced
30ml/2 tbsp sesame seeds, toasted
2 spring onions (scallions), thinly sliced diagonally and fresh coriander (cilantro) leaves, to garnish

For the dressing

45ml/3 tbsp sherry vinegar
75ml/5 tbsp soy sauce
60ml/4 tbsp sesame oil
90ml/6 tbsp light olive oil
1 garlic clove, finely chopped
5ml/1 tsp grated fresh root ginger
salt and freshly ground black pepper

1 Make the dressing by mixing all the ingredients in a small bowl and whisking them together.

2 Bring a large pan of lightly salted water to the boil and cook the noodles briefly until they are just tender, stirring occasionally. Drain, rinse under cold water and drain again. Tip into a large bowl.

3 Add the vegetables to the noodles. Pour in about half the dressing, then toss the mixture well and check the seasoning.

4 Preheat a wok, then swirl in the oil. When it is hot, add the chicken and stir-fry for 3 minutes, or until cooked and golden. Remove the wok from the heat. Add the sesame seeds and drizzle in the remaining dressing.

5 Arrange the noodle mixture on serving plates. Spoon the chicken on top. Sprinkle with the spring onions and coriander.

Thai Noodle Salad

Coconut milk and sesame oil give the dressing for this colourful noodle salad an unusual, nutty flavour.

Serves 4–6

350g/12oz somen noodles
1 large carrot, cut into thin strips
225g/8oz asparagus, trimmed and cut into 4cm/1½in lengths
1 red (bell) pepper, seeded and cut into fine strips
115g/4oz/1 cup mangetouts (snow peas), halved
115g/4oz/⅔ cup baby corn cobs, halved lengthways
115g/4oz/2 cups beansprouts
115g/4oz can water chestnuts, drained and thinly sliced
lime wedges, chopped roasted peanuts and fresh coriander (cilantro) leaves, to garnish

For the dressing

45ml/3 tbsp coarsely torn fresh basil
75ml/5 tbsp coarsely chopped fresh mint
250ml/8fl oz/1 cup coconut milk
30ml/2 tbsp dark sesame oil
15ml/1 tbsp grated fresh root ginger
2 garlic cloves, finely chopped
juice of 1 lime
2 spring onions (scallions), finely chopped
salt and cayenne pepper

1 First, make the dressing. Mix the basil, mint, coconut milk, sesame oil, ginger, garlic, lime juice and spring onions in a bowl. Whisk until well combined, then season to taste with salt and cayenne pepper.

2 Bring a large pan of lightly salted water to the boil and cook the noodles until they are just tender. Drain, rinse under cold water and drain again. Tip into a large bowl.

3 Cook all the vegetables in separate pans of boiling lightly salted water until they are tender, but still crisp. As each vegetable cooks, drain it, plunge it into cold water and drain well again.

4 Add the vegetables and dressing to the bowl of noodles and toss thoroughly. Divide the noodle salad among individual serving plates and garnish with the lime wedges, peanuts and coriander leaves.

Sesame Noodle Salad

Hot peanuts unite deliciously with cold noodles.

Serves 4

350g/12oz dried egg noodles
2 carrots, cut into thin batons
½ cucumber, peeled and cubed
115g/4oz celeriac, cut into thin batons
6 spring onions (scallions), thinly sliced
8 drained canned water chestnuts, thinly sliced
175g/6oz/3 cups beansprouts
1 small fresh green chilli, seeded and finely chopped
30ml/2 tbsp sesame seeds and 115g/4oz/1 cup peanuts, to serve

For the dressing

15ml/1 tbsp dark soy sauce
15ml/1 tbsp light soy sauce
15ml/1 tbsp clear honey
15ml/1 tbsp dry sherry
15ml/1 tbsp sesame oil

1 Preheat the oven to 200°C/400°F/Gas 6. Bring a large pan of lightly salted water to the boil and cook the noodles until they are just tender. Drain, rinse under cold water and drain again. Tip them into a large bowl and add all the prepared vegetables.

2 Make the dressing by mixing all the ingredients in a small bowl. Pour over the noodle mixture and toss until well mixed. Divide the salad among four plates or dishes.

3 Place the sesame seeds and peanuts on separate baking sheets. Place the sesame seeds in the oven for 5 minutes and the peanuts for 10 minutes, until evenly browned. Sprinkle the sesame seeds and peanuts evenly over each portion and serve.

Japanese Summer Salad

This unusual salad will be a talking point among guests.

Serves 6

6 dried shiitake mushrooms, soaked in hot water for 10 minutes
45ml/3 tbsp mirin
120ml/4fl oz/½ cup dashi
18 raw tiger prawns (jumbo shrimp)
1 thin slice fresh root ginger
15ml/1 tbsp shoyu
225g/8oz somen noodles
salt
watercress sprigs, to garnish
30ml/2 tbsp grated fresh root ginger and 30ml/2 tbsp wasabi paste, to serve

1 Put the mushrooms and soaking liquid in a small pan, add 30ml/2 tbsp of the mirin and simmer for 20 minutes, until the liquid has evaporated. Remove with a slotted spoon, cut off the stalks and cut the caps in half without squeezing out the liquid.
2 Bring the dashi to the boil in a small pan. Add the prawns and ginger, cover and remove from the heat. Set aside for 5 minutes. Strain the dashi into a bowl. Stir in the shoyu and remaining mirin. Peel the prawns.
3 Bring a pan of salted water to the boil and cook the noodles until just tender. Drain and rinse under cold water. Divide the noodles among glass bowls, add two to three ice cubes and 120ml/4fl oz/½ cup iced water to each. Arrange three prawns and two mushroom halves on top. Garnish with watercress. Serve with ginger, wasabi paste and the dashi dipping sauce.

QUICK & EASY

One of pasta's many charms is the speed with which it cooks. However, while this is a flying start, it is no help to the cook in a hurry unless the sauce to go with it can be prepared just as quickly. This chapter demonstrates that fast food can be fine food. While the pasta is boiling, the scrumptious sauces can be prepared to produce a family supper, an easy lunch or even a dinner-party appetizer in a matter of minutes. Even the most enthusiastic cook knows those occasions when the mere thought of preparing supper is almost too much effort and inspiration has fled. This chapter provides the answer with a mouth-watering choice of no-fuss, easy-cook, high-speed recipes based on store-cupboard (pantry) ingredients. These are also the perfect solution to how to entertain unexpected visitors – just pop into the kitchen and rustle up Spaghetti with Bacon & Onion or Farfalle with Tuna. Other recipes will soon become favourite fixtures in the midweek menu. Cheese, shellfish, and fresh vegetables – all ingredients than can be ready in a flash – combine superbly with pasta or noodles to produce almost instantaneous meals. When you serve a colourful dish of Indonesian Bamie Goreng or bowls of dramatic black Squid Ink Pasta with Ricotta – both of which taste as wonderful as they look – no one will believe that you haven't spent hours slaving over a hot stove.

Orecchiette with Anchovies & Broccoli

Puglia, in southern Italy, specializes in imaginative pasta and vegetable combinations. Cooking the pasta in the water used for boiling the broccoli, then using some of it in the sauce, intensifies the flavour.

Serves 6

800g/1¾ lb broccoli
450g/1lb/4 cups dried orecchiette or penne
90ml/6 tbsp olive oil
3 garlic cloves, finely chopped
6 drained canned anchovy fillets in oil
salt and freshly ground black pepper

1 Cut off the broccoli florets and divide them into sprigs. Peel the stems, then cut them into 5cm/2in lengths, discarding the woody parts.

2 Bring a large pan of water to the boil. Drop in the broccoli stems, bring back to the boil and cook for 3 minutes, then add the florets and boil for a further 3 minutes. Lift out all the broccoli with a slotted spoon and transfer it to a serving bowl. Do not discard the cooking water.

3 Add a little salt to the water used for cooking the broccoli. Bring it back to the boil. Drop in the pasta, stir well and cook until it is *al dente*.

4 While the pasta is boiling, heat the oil in a small frying pan. Add the garlic and cook over a low heat for 2–3 minutes. Add the anchovy fillets. Using a fork, mash the anchovies and garlic to a paste. Cook for 3–4 minutes more.

5 Before draining the pasta, ladle about 175ml/6fl oz/¾ cup of the cooking water over the broccoli. Drain the pasta and add it to the bowl, with the hot anchovy and garlic mixture. Mix well, season with pepper, if necessary, and serve.

Pasta with Spinach & Anchovy Sauce

Deliciously earthy, this quick and easy dish would make a good appetizer or light supper dish.

Serves 4

900g/2lb fresh spinach or 500g/1¼lb frozen leaf spinach, thawed
450g/1lb dried capelli d'angelo
60ml/4 tbsp olive oil
45ml/3 tbsp pine nuts
2 garlic cloves, crushed
6 drained canned anchovy fillets or whole salted anchovies, chopped
butter, for tossing the pasta
salt

1 Remove the tough stalks from the spinach, wash the leaves thoroughly in a colander and place them in a large pan with only the water that still clings to them. Cover with a lid and cook over a high heat, shaking the pan occasionally, until the spinach has just wilted and is bright green. Drain well and set aside until required.

2 Bring a pan of lightly salted water to the boil. Add the pasta and cook until it is *al dente*.

3 Meanwhile, heat the oil in a pan, add the pine nuts and fry until golden. Remove with a slotted spoon and set aside. Add the garlic to the oil in the pan and fry until golden. Add the anchovies to the pan.

4 Stir in the spinach and cook for 2–3 minutes, or until it is hot. Stir in the pine nuts. Drain the pasta, toss it in a little butter and turn it into a warmed serving bowl. Top with the sauce, fork it through roughly and serve.

Variation
Add some sultanas (golden raisins), if you like. Their sweetness will counteract the salty flavour of the anchovies.

Farfalle with Tuna

A quick and simple dish that makes a good weekday supper if you have canned tomatoes and tuna in your kitchen stores.

Serves 4
30ml/2 tbsp olive oil
1 small onion, finely chopped
1 garlic clove, finely chopped
400g/14oz can chopped tomatoes
45ml/3 tbsp dry white wine
8–10 pitted black olives, cut into rings
10ml/2 tsp chopped fresh oregano or 5ml/1 tsp dried, plus extra fresh oregano to garnish
400g/14oz/3½ cups dried farfalle
175g/6oz can tuna in olive oil, drained and flaked
salt and freshly ground black pepper

1 Heat the olive oil in a large, heavy pan. Add the onion and garlic and cook gently, stirring occasionally, for 2–3 minutes, until the onion is soft and golden.

2 Stir in the tomatoes. Bring to the boil, then add the white wine and simmer for 1–2 minutes. Stir in the olives and oregano and season with salt and pepper to taste. Cover and cook for 20–25 minutes, stirring occasionally.

3 Meanwhile, bring a large pan of lightly salted water to the boil. Add the pasta and cook until *al dente*.

4 Add the tuna to the sauce with about 60ml/4 tbsp of the water used for cooking the pasta. Taste and adjust the seasoning, if necessary.

5 Drain the cooked pasta well and tip it into a warmed large serving bowl. Pour the tuna sauce over the top and toss to mix. Serve immediately, garnished with oregano sprigs.

Spaghetti with Tuna & Anchovies

This simple pasta dish is fresh, light and full of flavour. Serve it as soon as it is cooked to enjoy it at its very best.

Serves 4
300g/11oz dried spaghetti
30ml/2 tbsp olive oil
6 ripe Italian plum tomatoes, chopped
5ml/1 tsp granulated sugar
50g/2oz jar anchovies in olive oil, drained
about 60ml/4 tbsp dry white wine
200g/7oz can tuna in olive oil, drained
50g/2oz/½ cup pitted black olives, quartered lengthways
125g/4½ oz packet mozzarella cheese, drained and diced
salt and freshly ground black pepper
fresh basil leaves, to garnish

1 Bring a large pan of lightly salted water to the boil, add the pasta and cook until it is *al dente*.

2 Meanwhile, heat the oil in a medium pan. Add the tomatoes and sugar and season with pepper to taste. Toss over a medium heat for a few minutes, until the tomatoes have softened and the juices run.

3 Using kitchen scissors, snip a few anchovies at a time into the pan of tomatoes. Add the wine, tuna and olives and stir once or twice until they are evenly mixed into the sauce.

4 Add the mozzarella and heat through without stirring. Taste and add salt, if necessary.

5 Drain the pasta and tip it into a warmed bowl. Pour the sauce over, toss gently and sprinkle with the basil leaves to garnish. Serve immediately.

Cook's Tip

Plum tomatoes have firmer flesh and are less watery than many other varieties. Look for sun-ripened specimens, which will be sweeter and have more flavour than glasshouse tomatoes.

Chilli, Anchovy & Tomato Pasta

The sauce for this tasty pasta dish packs a punch, thanks to the robust flavours of red chillies, anchovies and capers.

Serves 4

45ml/3 tbsp olive oil
2 garlic cloves, crushed
2 fresh red chillies, seeded and chopped
6 drained canned anchovy fillets
675g/1½lb ripe tomatoes, peeled, seeded and chopped
30ml/2 tbsp sun-dried tomato purée (paste)
30ml/2 tbsp drained capers
115g/4oz/1 cup pitted black olives, coarsely chopped
350g/12oz/3 cups dried penne
salt and freshly ground black pepper
chopped fresh basil, to garnish

1 Heat the oil in a pan and fry the garlic and chilli over a low heat for 2–3 minutes.

2 Add the anchovies, mashing them with a fork, then stir in the tomatoes, sun-dried tomato purée, capers and olives. Add salt and pepper to taste. Simmer gently, uncovered, for 20 minutes, stirring occasionally.

3 Meanwhile, bring a large pan of lightly salted water to the boil and add the penne. Cook until *al dente*.

4 Drain the pasta, return it to the clean pan and add the sauce. Mix thoroughly, tip into a heated serving dish, garnish with the basil and serve immediately.

Cook's Tip

If ripe well-flavoured tomatoes are not available, use 2 x 400g/14oz cans chopped tomatoes. If the chillies are a very hot variety, use only one.

Macaroni with Anchovies & Mixed Vegetables

This southern Italian dish is colourful and full of flavour.

Serves 4

175g/6oz cauliflower florets, cut into small sprigs
175g/6oz broccoli florets, cut into small sprigs
350g/12oz/3 cups short-cut macaroni
45ml/3 tbsp extra virgin olive oil
1 onion, finely chopped
45ml/3 tbsp pine nuts
1 sachet of saffron powder, dissolved in 15ml/1 tbsp warm water
15–30ml/1–2 tbsp raisins
30ml/2 tbsp sun-dried tomato purée (paste)
4 drained canned anchovies in olive oil, chopped, plus extra anchovies, to serve (optional)
salt and freshly ground black pepper
freshly grated Pecorino cheese, to serve

1 Bring a large pan of lightly salted water to the boil and cook the cauliflower sprigs for 3 minutes. Add the broccoli and boil for 2 minutes more. Remove the vegetables from the pan with a large slotted spoon and set them aside.

2 Reboil the water, add the pasta and cook until it is *al dente*.

3 Meanwhile, heat the olive oil in a large, shallow pan and fry the onion over a low heat, for 2–3 minutes, or until golden. Add the pine nuts, broccoli, cauliflower and saffron water.

4 Stir in the raisins, sun-dried tomato purée and a couple of ladlefuls of the pasta cooking water until the vegetable mixture has the consistency of a sauce. Finally, add plenty of pepper.

5 Stir well, cook for 1–2 minutes, then add the chopped anchovies. Drain the pasta and tip it into the vegetable mixture. Toss well, then taste for seasoning and add salt if necessary.

6 Serve the pasta in four warmed bowls, sprinkling each portion liberally with freshly grated Pecorino. If you like the flavour of anchovies, add two whole anchovies to each serving.

Farfalle with Prawns

Cream sauces are not always the best way to serve fish with pasta. This simple fresh prawn sauce allows the distinctive flavour of the shellfish to shine.

Serves 4
225g/8oz/2 cups dried farfalle
115g/4oz/½ cup butter
2 garlic cloves, crushed
45ml/3 tbsp chopped fresh parsley, plus extra, to garnish
350g/12oz/3 cups cooked peeled prawns (shrimp)
salt and freshly ground black pepper

1 Bring a large pan of lightly salted water to the boil. Add the pasta and cook until *al dente*.

2 Meanwhile, melt the butter in a large, heavy pan. Add the garlic and fresh parsley, and cook over a low heat, stirring, for 2 minutes. Toss in the prawns and sauté, stirring occasionally, for 4 minutes.

3 Drain the pasta and return it to the clean pan. Stir in the prawn mixture. Season to taste. Serve immediately in warmed shallow bowls. Garnish with the extra chopped parsley.

Variation
For extra colour, fry one diced red (bell) pepper with the garlic and parsley. Add some chopped red onion too, if you like, but avoid adding too much, as it might overwhelm the delicate flavour of the prawns (shrimp). A splash of dry white vermouth, added with the prawns, would work well.

Cook's Tip
For the best flavour and texture, buy prawns (shrimp) with their shells on and peel them yourself. Ready-peeled and frozen prawns tend to become rather mushy.

Pasta with Prawns & Petits Pois

A small amount of saffron in the sauce gives this dish a lovely golden colour.

Serves 4
400g/14oz/3½ cups dried farfalle
45ml/3 tbsp olive oil
25g/1oz/2 tbsp butter
2 spring onions (scallions), chopped
225g/8oz/2 cups frozen petits pois (baby peas), thawed
250ml/8fl oz/1 cup dry white wine
a few saffron threads
350g/12oz/3 cups cooked peeled prawns (shrimp)
salt
30ml/2 tbsp chopped fresh dill, to serve

1 Bring a large pan of lightly salted water to the boil. Add the pasta and cook until *al dente*.

2 Meanwhile, heat the oil and butter in a large, heavy frying pan and sauté the spring onions until soft and translucent. Add the peas and cook for 2–3 minutes.

3 Stir the white wine and saffron into the spring onion mixture. Increase the heat and cook until the wine has reduced to about half. Gently stir in the prawns, cover the pan and reduce the heat to low.

4 Drain the pasta and return it to the clean pan. Add the prawn sauce. Stir over a high heat for 2–3 minutes, coating the pasta with the sauce. Sprinkle with the dill and serve.

Cook's Tip
Prawns (shrimp) vary in size and colour, offering a wide variety of choice. Mediterranean prawns – the most authentic for this dish – grow to 20–23cm/8–9in, are brown before cooking and bright red afterwards. Pale brown, deep-water prawns, found in both the Mediterranean and the Atlantic, and blue-brown Pacific prawns are much larger. Both turn bright pink when cooked. Greenland prawns are relatively small and pink.

Tagliolini with Clam, Leek & Tomato Sauce

Canned or bottled clams make this a speedy sauce for cooks in a hurry.

Serves 4

350g/12oz dried tagliolini
25g/1oz/2 tbsp butter
2 leeks, thinly sliced
150ml/ 1/4 pint/ 2/3 cup dry white wine
4 tomatoes, peeled, seeded and chopped
250g/9oz can or jar clams in brine, drained
30ml/2 tbsp chopped fresh basil
60ml/4 tbsp crème fraîche
salt and freshly ground black pepper

1 Bring a large pan of lightly salted water to the boil and cook the pasta until it is *al dente*.

2 Meanwhile, melt the butter in a small pan and fry the leeks for about 5 minutes, until softened. Add the wine and tomatoes. Cook over a high heat until reduced by half.

3 Lower the heat, stir in the clams, basil and crème fraîche, and season with salt and pepper to taste. Heat through gently without boiling.

4 Drain the pasta, return it to the clean pan and add the sauce. Toss well to mix. Serve immediately.

Variations

Try salmon-flavoured tagliolini for an attractive presentation. It looks good with the tomato-based clam sauce and intensifies the shellfish flavour. Alternatively, for a very dramatic presentation, use a mixture of plain pasta and black tagliolini flavoured with squid or cuttlefish ink.

Spaghetti with Red Wine Clam Sauce

Small sweet clams make this a delicately succulent spaghetti sauce, while fresh chilli gives it a kick.

Serves 4

90ml/6 tbsp olive oil
1 onion, finely chopped
1/2 fresh red chilli, seeded and finely chopped
2 garlic cloves, crushed
2 x 400g/14oz cans chopped tomatoes
120ml/4fl oz/ 1/2 cup red wine
2 x 400g/14oz cans clams in brine, drained
45ml/3 tbsp chopped fresh parsley
450g/1lb dried spaghetti
salt and freshly ground black pepper

1 Heat the olive oil in a heavy pan and add the onion, chilli and garlic. Cook over a low to medium heat, stirring occasionally, for about 5 minutes, until the onion is soft and translucent.

2 Add the chopped tomatoes and red wine and bring to the boil. Lower the heat and simmer gently for about 10 minutes, until the sauce is thick and flavoursome. Stir in the canned clams and half the parsley. Season to taste with salt and pepper and heat through.

3 Meanwhile, bring a large pan of lightly salted water to the boil and cook the pasta until *al dente*.

4 Drain the pasta and turn it into a warmed serving dish. Pour over the sauce, sprinkle with the remaining chopped parsley and serve immediately.

Cook's Tip

Use more chilli if you like. Clams have a much more robust flavour than mussels and other shellfish, so they can take quite a hot sauce. For those who like their food fiery, use chilli-flavoured pasta instead of plain.

Tagliatelle with Brandied Scallops

Scallops and brandy make this a relatively expensive dish, but it is so delicious that you will find it well worth the cost.

Serves 4

200g/7oz shelled scallops, sliced
30ml/2 tbsp plain (all-purpose) flour
40g/1½oz/3 tbsp butter
2 spring onions (scallions), thinly sliced
½–1 small fresh red chilli, seeded and very finely chopped
30ml/2 tbsp finely chopped fresh flat leaf parsley
60ml/4 tbsp brandy
105ml/7 tbsp fish stock
275g/10oz fresh spinach-flavoured tagliatelle
salt and freshly ground black pepper

1 Toss the scallops in the flour, then shake off the excess. Bring a large pan of lightly salted water to the boil.

2 Meanwhile, melt the butter in a large shallow pan. Add the spring onions, chilli and half the parsley. Fry over a medium heat, stirring frequently, for 1–2 minutes. Add the scallops and toss over the heat for 1–2 minutes.

3 Pour the brandy over the scallops, then set it alight with a match or taper. As soon as the flames have died down, stir in the fish stock and season with salt and pepper to taste. Mix well. Simmer for 2–3 minutes, then cover the pan and remove it from the heat.

4 Add the pasta to the boiling water and cook until *al dente*. Drain, add to the sauce and toss over a medium heat. Serve in warmed bowls. Sprinkle with the remaining parsley.

Cook's Tip

Buy fresh scallops, with their corals if possible. Fresh scallops have a better texture and flavour than frozen scallops, which tend to be watery.

Squid Ink Pasta with Ricotta

Black pasta looks very dramatic and is the perfect vehicle for the creamy sauce. This dish would make a perfect appetizer for a dinner party, in which case, it would serve six.

Serves 4

300g/11oz dried squid ink spaghetti
60ml/4 tbsp ricotta cheese
60ml/4 tbsp extra virgin olive oil
1 small fresh red chilli, seeded and finely chopped
1 small handful fresh basil leaves
salt and freshly ground black pepper

1 Bring a pan of lightly salted water to the boil and cook the pasta until it is *al dente*.

2 Meanwhile, put the ricotta in a bowl, add salt and pepper to taste and use a little of the hot water from the pasta pan to mix it to a smooth, creamy consistency.

3 Drain the pasta. Heat the olive oil gently in the clean pan and return the pasta to it with the chilli. Season with salt and pepper to taste. Toss quickly over a high heat to combine.

4 Divide the pasta equally among four warmed bowls, then top with the ricotta. Sprinkle with the basil leaves and serve immediately. Each diner then tosses his or her own portion of pasta and cheese.

Cook's Tips

- *If you are not keen on the flavour of squid ink, use another coloured pasta, such as green (spinach-flavoured) pasta, red (tomato-flavoured) pasta, brown (mushroom- or porcini-flavoured) pasta or simple multi-coloured pasta instead.*
- *Do make sure that you use extra virgin olive oil, as this has the best flavour and the lowest acidity. The olive oil forms an integral part of the dish, and poorer quality oils would be likely to spoil the delicate and subtle flavour.*

Fusilli with Chicken & Tomato Sauce

For a speedy supper, serve this dish with a salad.

Serves 4

15ml/1 tbsp olive oil
1 onion, chopped
1 carrot, chopped
1 garlic clove, chopped
400g/14oz can chopped tomatoes
15ml/1 tbsp tomato purée (paste)
150ml/ ¼ pint/ ⅔ cup chicken stock
350g/12oz/3 cups dried fusilli
50g/2oz/ ½ cup drained sun-dried tomatoes in olive oil, chopped
225g/8oz skinless, boneless chicken breast portions, diagonally sliced
salt
fresh mint sprigs, to garnish

1 Heat the oil in a large frying pan and fry the onion and carrot for 5 minutes, stirring occasionally.

2 Stir in the garlic, canned tomatoes, tomato purée and stock. Bring to the boil, then lower the heat and simmer for about 10 minutes, stirring occasionally.

3 Meanwhile, bring a large pan of lightly salted water to the boil and cook the pasta until *al dente*.

4 Pour the sauce into a blender or food processor and process until smooth. Return it to the pan and stir in the sun-dried tomatoes and chicken. Bring to the boil, then simmer for 10 minutes, until the chicken is cooked.

5 Drain the pasta and return it to the clean pan. Toss it with the sauce. Serve in heated bowls, garnished with the mint.

Cook's Tip
If you have a hand-held food processor, simply purée the sauce in the pan.

Chicken & Pasta Balti

Of course, this is not a traditional Balti dish, as pasta is seldom served in India or Pakistan, but nonetheless it is delicious.

Serves 4–6

75g/3oz/ ¾ cup dried conchiglie
60ml/4 tbsp corn oil
4 curry leaves
4 whole dried red chillies
1 large onion, sliced
1–2 garlic cloves, crushed
5ml/1 tsp chilli powder
2.5cm/1in piece of fresh root ginger, grated
5ml/1 tsp crushed pomegranate seeds
5ml/1 tsp salt
2 tomatoes, chopped
175g/6oz skinless, boneless chicken, cubed
275g/10oz can chickpeas, drained
115g/4oz/ ⅔ cup drained canned sweetcorn
50g/2oz/ ⅓ cup mangetouts (snow peas), sliced diagonally

1 Bring a large pan of lightly salted water to the boil. Cook the pasta until it is *al dente*, then drain it, rinse it under hot water and drain it again.

2 Heat the oil in a deep frying pan and fry the curry leaves, whole dried chillies and onion for 5 minutes. Add the garlic, chilli powder, ginger, pomegranate seeds, salt and tomatoes. Stir-fry for 3 minutes.

3 Add the chicken, chickpeas, sweetcorn and mangetouts to the onion mixture. Cook over a medium heat, stirring constantly, for 5 minutes.

4 Tip in the pasta and stir well. Cook for 7–10 minutes more, or until the chicken is cooked through. Transfer to warmed individual bowls and serve immediately.

Cook's Tip
Using coloured pasta shells makes this dish look especially attractive and appetizing.

Spaghetti with Bacon & Onion

This easy dish can be made quickly from ingredients that are almost always to hand.

Serves 6
30ml/2 tbsp olive oil
115g/4oz rindless unsmoked streaky (fatty) bacon rashers (strips) cut into thin batons
1 small onion, finely chopped
120ml/4fl oz/ ½ cup dry white wine
450g/1lb tomatoes, chopped
1.5ml/ ¼ tsp thyme leaves
500g/1 ¼lb dried spaghetti
salt and freshly ground black pepper
freshly grated Parmesan cheese, to serve

1 Heat the oil in a heavy frying pan. Add the bacon and onion, and cook over a medium heat, stirring occasionally, for about 8–10 minutes, until the onion is golden and the bacon has rendered its fat and is beginning to brown.

2 Add the wine to the bacon mixture, raise the heat and cook rapidly until the liquid has evaporated. Stir in the tomatoes and thyme and season with salt and pepper to taste. Cover, and cook over a moderate heat for 10–15 minutes.

3 Meanwhile, bring a large pan of lightly salted water to the boil and cook the pasta until it is *al dente*. Drain, return to the clean pan and toss with the sauce. Serve with the grated Parmesan.

Variations
This recipe is easily adapted to use whatever ingredients you have in your store cupboard (pantry) and refrigerator. You could try adding one finely chopped carrot or celery stick with the onion in step 1. For a spicy flavour, add a pinch of chilli powder or cayenne pepper instead of black pepper in step 2.

Pasta with Fresh Tomato & Smoky Bacon Sauce

This is a wonderful pasta sauce to prepare in mid-summer when the tomatoes are ripe and sweet.

Serves 4
900g/2lb ripe tomatoes
50g/2oz/ ¼ cup butter
6 rindless smoked streaky bacon rashers, chopped
1 medium onion, chopped
15ml/1 tbsp chopped fresh oregano
450g/1lb/4 cups dried pasta shapes
salt and freshly ground black pepper
fresh marjoram sprigs, to garnish
freshly grated Parmesan cheese, to serve

1 Cut a cross in the blossom end of each tomato. Plunge them into boiling water for 1 minute, then into cold water. Slip off the skins, peeling them back from the crosses. Cut the tomatoes in half, remove the seeds and cores, and roughly chop the flesh.

2 Melt the butter in a pan. Add the bacon and fry until lightly browned. Add the onion and cook gently for 5 minutes until softened.

3 Add the tomatoes and oregano, and season with salt and pepper to taste. Simmer gently for 10 minutes.

4 Bring a large pan of lightly salted water to the boil and cook the pasta until *al dente*. Drain, return to the clean pan and toss with the sauce. Ladle into warmed bowls. Garnish with marjoram sprigs and serve with grated Parmesan cheese.

Stir-fried Bacon & Pak Choi with Pasta

Quick, easy and tasty, this is an ideal dish for those hectic nights when everyone is in a hurry.

Serves 4
350g/12oz/3 cups dried spaghettini
15ml/1 tbsp vegetable oil
4 rindless streaky (fatty) bacon rashers (strips), cut into strips
2 leeks, sliced
1 celeriac, peeled and diced
1 head pak choi (bok choy), stems and leaves chopped separately
soy sauce
salt

1 Bring a large pan of lightly salted water to the boil and cook the pasta until *al dente*.
2 Meanwhile, preheat a wok. Add the oil and stir-fry the bacon with the leeks until the bacon is beginning to become crisp.
3 Add the celeriac and pak choi stems and toss over the heat for 3–4 minutes.
4 Stir in the pak choi leaves, add a generous drizzle of soy sauce, cover the wok with a tight-fitting lid and steam the leaves for 2–3 minutes.
5 Drain the pasta, add it to the stir-fried ingredients and toss lightly. Serve immediately, with extra soy sauce if needed.

Linguine with Smoked Ham & Artichokes

Canned artichoke hearts are a wonderful convenience ingredient and taste superb in this simple sauce. Use bacon if you haven't got any smoked ham.

Serves 4

350g/12oz dried linguine
45ml/3 tbsp olive oil
1 onion, chopped
2 garlic cloves, chopped
400g/14oz can artichoke hearts, drained and sliced
225g/8oz smoked ham, diced
30ml/2 tbsp chopped fresh basil
15ml/1 tbsp herb vinegar
150ml/ ¼ pint/ ⅔ cup sour cream
salt and freshly ground black pepper
fresh mint sprigs, to garnish

1 Bring a large pan of lightly salted water to the boil and cook the pasta until *al dente*.

2 Meanwhile, heat the oil in a heavy frying pan. Add the onion and garlic and fry over a medium heat, stirring occasionally, for 5 minutes until the onion has softened.

3 Add the artichoke hearts and toss gently over the heat for 2 minutes. Try not to break them up.

4 Add the ham and basil and fry, stirring constantly, for about 2 minutes. Pour in the herb vinegar, season with salt and pepper to taste and heat through. Stir in the sour cream and heat through again, stirring constantly.

5 Drain the pasta and return it to the clean pan. Add the sauce and toss to coat. Spoon into a warmed bowl, garnish with the mint sprigs and serve immediately.

Variation

Smoked chicken, poussin or turkey also work well in this delicious recipe.

Prosciutto Pasta with Asparagus

Make this dish with young asparagus, when it first comes into the shops in the late spring. You can also use sprue, the first thinnings of asparagus, which are very thin and often cheaper.

Serves 4

350g/12oz dried tagliatelle
25g/1oz/2 tbsp butter
15ml/1 tbsp olive oil
225g/8oz fresh asparagus tips
1 garlic clove, chopped
115g/4oz prosciutto, cut into strips
30ml/2 tbsp chopped fresh sage
150ml/ ¼ pint/ ⅔ cup single (light) cream
115g/4oz double Gloucester or Cheddar cheese, grated
115g/4oz Gruyère cheese, grated
salt and freshly ground black pepper
fresh sage sprigs, to garnish

1 Bring a large pan of lightly salted water to the boil and cook the pasta until it is *al dente*.

2 Melt the butter in the oil in a heavy frying pan. Add the asparagus tips and fry gently over a low heat, stirring occasionally, for about 5 minutes, until almost tender.

3 Stir in the garlic and ham and fry for 1 minute, then add the chopped sage leaves and fry for 1 minute more.

4 Pour in the cream, bring to the boil, then lower the heat and stir in the double Gloucester or Cheddar and the Gruyère. Simmer gently, stirring occasionally, until the cheeses have melted. Season with salt and pepper to taste.

5 Drain the pasta and return it to the clean pan. Add the sauce and toss to coat. Serve immediately in warmed bowls, garnished with the fresh sage.

Tagliatelle with Leeks & Prosciutto

The mild, slightly sweet flavour of leeks makes them the perfect partner for prosciutto and pasta in this prettily coloured dish. For the best effect, use a mixture of green and white tagliatelle if possible.

Serves 4

40g/1½ oz/3 tbsp butter
5 leeks, sliced
225g/8oz fresh or dried tagliatelle, preferably green and white
20ml/4 tsp dry sherry
30ml/2 tbsp lemon juice
10ml/2 tsp chopped fresh basil
115–150g/4–5oz prosciutto, torn into strips
175g/6oz/¾ cup fromage frais or cream cheese
salt and freshly ground black pepper
fresh basil leaves and thin shavings of Parmesan cheese, to garnish

1 Melt the butter in a large, heavy pan, add the leeks and fry over a gentle heat, stirring occasionally, for 3–4 minutes, until tender but not too soft.

2 Meanwhile, bring a large pan of lightly salted water to the boil and cook the tagliatelle until it is *al dente*.

3 Stir the sherry, lemon juice and chopped basil into the leek mixture. Season with salt and pepper to taste, and cook for 1–2 minutes so that the flavours blend.

4 Add the strips of prosciutto and the fromage frais or cream cheese, stir and cook over a low heat for about 1–2 minutes, until heated through.

5 Drain the pasta and return it to the clean pan. Pour the leek and prosciutto mixture on top and mix lightly together. Spoon into warmed individual bowls and garnish each serving with fresh basil leaves. Top with shavings of Parmesan cheese and serve immediately.

Tagliatelle with Prosciutto & Parmesan

A really simple dish, prepared in minutes from the best ingredients.

Serves 4

115g/4oz prosciutto
450g/1lb dried tagliatelle
75g/3oz/6 tbsp butter
50g/2oz/⅔ cup freshly grated Parmesan cheese
salt and freshly ground black pepper
a few fresh sage leaves, to garnish

1 Cut the prosciutto into strips, making them the same width as the tagliatelle. Bring a large pan of lightly salted water to the boil and cook the pasta until it is *al dente*.

2 Meanwhile, melt the butter in a pan, stir in the prosciutto strips and heat them through, but do not fry.

3 Drain the pasta and pile it into a warm serving dish. Sprinkle with the Parmesan and pour over the buttery prosciutto. Season with pepper, garnish with the sage leaves and serve.

Variation

This dish also works well with thin strips of peeled red (bell) peppers. Grill (broil) the peppers under a medium heat until they are blistered. Place in a bowl and cover with clear film (plastic wrap) until cool enough to handle. Peel off the skins, discard the seeds and cut the flesh into strips the same width as the tagliatelle. Warm them in the butter with the prosciutto.

Penne with Salame Napoletano

Spicy sausage tossed in cheesy tomato sauce is delicious with pasta.

Serves 4

350g/12oz/3 cups dried penne
30ml/2 tbsp olive oil
225g/8oz salame napoletano or chorizo sausage, sliced diagonally
450g/1lb ripe tomatoes, peeled and chopped
1 garlic clove, chopped
30ml/2 tbsp chopped fresh flat leaf parsley, plus extra to garnish
grated rind of 1 lemon
50g/2oz/⅔ cup freshly grated Parmesan cheese
salt and freshly ground black pepper

1 Bring a large pan of lightly salted water to the boil and cook the pasta until *al dente*.

2 Meanwhile, heat the oil in a heavy frying pan. Add the salame or chorizo and fry over a medium heat, stirring occasionally, for 5 minutes, until browned.

3 Add the tomatoes, garlic, parsley and grated lemon rind. Heat through, stirring constantly, for 1 minute, then stir in the Parmesan and season with salt and pepper to taste.

4 Drain the pasta thoroughly and return it to the clean pan. Add the sauce and toss to coat. Serve in warmed bowls, garnished with the extra parsley.

Cook's Tip
Salame napoletano is a spicy Italian sausage, made with a mixture of pork and beef and flavoured with red and black pepper. It is quite fiery, so if you prefer a milder flavour, try salame fiorentino – a pure pork sausage – or genovese – a mixture of pork and veal. Look for salame at Italian delicatessens. If you are unable to locate it, use mild or hot Spanish chorizo sausage instead.

Spirali with Wild Mushrooms & Chorizo Sauce

The delicious combination of wild mushrooms and spicy sausage make this a tempting supper dish.

Serves 4

350g/12oz/3 cups dried spirali
60ml/4 tbsp olive oil
1 garlic clove, chopped
1 celery stick, chopped
225g/8oz chorizo sausage, sliced
225g/8oz/3 cups mixed wild mushrooms, such as oyster, brown cap, shiitake
15ml/1 tbsp lemon juice
30ml/2 tbsp chopped fresh oregano
salt and freshly ground black pepper
finely chopped fresh parsley, to garnish

1 Bring a large pan of lightly salted water to the boil and cook the pasta until it is *al dente*.

2 Meanwhile, heat the oil in a heavy frying pan. Add the garlic and celery, and fry over a medium heat, stirring occasionally, for 5 minutes, until the celery has softened.

3 Add the chorizo and cook, stirring occasionally, for 5 minutes, until browned, then stir in the wild mushrooms. Cook for 4 minutes, stirring occasionally until slightly softened.

4 Stir in the lemon juice and oregano. Season with salt and pepper to taste and heat through.

5 Drain the pasta thoroughly and turn it into a warmed serving bowl. Toss with the sauce to coat. Serve immediately, garnished with fresh parsley.

Cook's Tip
Use any combination of wild mushrooms for this flavoursome sauce or even a mixture of wild and cultivated. Season the dish sparingly, as chorizo is quite peppery.

Spaghetti with Ham & Saffron

A quick and easy dish that makes a delicious midweek supper. The ingredients are all staples that you are likely to have to hand.

Serves 4

350g/12oz dried spaghetti
a few saffron threads
30ml/2 tbsp water
150g/5oz cooked ham, cut into thin batons
200ml/7fl oz/scant 1 cup double (heavy) cream
50g/2oz/⅔ cup freshly grated Parmesan cheese, plus extra to serve
2 egg yolks
salt and freshly ground black pepper

1 Bring a pan of lightly salted water to the boil and cook the pasta until it is *al dente*.

2 Meanwhile, put the saffron threads in a medium pan, add the water and bring to the boil immediately. Remove the pan from the heat and leave to stand for 5 minutes.

3 Add the ham to the pan containing the saffron. Stir in the cream and Parmesan, with a little salt and pepper. Heat gently, stirring constantly. When the cream starts to bubble around the edges, remove the pan from the heat and beat in the egg yolks.

4 Drain the pasta and return it to the clean pan. Immediately pour the sauce over and toss well. Serve in warmed bowls, with extra grated Parmesan handed separately.

Cook's Tip

Use a heavy pan for heating the cream so that it does not catch on the base. Make sure you beat the sauce immediately the eggs are added.

Tortellini with Ham

This is a very easy recipe; ideal for busy people as an after-work supper.

Serves 4

250g/9oz dried tortellini alla carne *(meat-filled tortellini)*
30ml/2 tbsp olive oil
1 shallot, finely chopped
115g/4oz cooked ham, diced
150ml/¼ pint/⅔ cup passata (bottled strained tomatoes)
150ml/¼ pint/⅔ cup water
120ml/4fl oz/½ cup double (heavy) cream
about 90g/3½ oz/generous 1 cup freshly grated Parmesan cheese
salt and freshly ground black pepper

1 Bring a pan of lightly salted water to the boil and cook the pasta until *al dente*.

2 Meanwhile, heat the oil in a heavy pan and cook the shallot over a low heat, stirring frequently, for 5 minutes, until softened. Add the ham and cook, stirring occasionally, until it darkens.

3 Add the passata and water. Stir well, then season with salt and pepper to taste. Bring to the boil, lower the heat and simmer the sauce until it has reduced slightly. Stir in the cream.

4 Drain the pasta well and add it to the sauce. Add a handful of grated Parmesan to the pan. Stir, toss well and taste for seasoning. Serve immediately in warmed bowls, topped with the remaining Parmesan.

Cook's Tip

Tortellini come with all sorts of fillings, and most would be suitable for this recipe. Meat-filled pasta includes mortadella sausage and pork, and chicken or turkey stuffings. A common vegetarian filling is spinach or chard, mixed with ricotta and Parmesan or Pecorino, sometimes with a flavouring of garlic and nutmeg. Four-cheese tortellini are also popular. A more unusual, but quite delicious, filling is a mixture of pumpkin, cheese, almonds, fruit and nutmeg.

Pepperoni Pasta

Add extra zip to pasta dishes, which can sometimes seem a little bland, with spicy pepperoni sausage.

Serves 4

275g/10oz/2½ cups dried penne
175g/6oz pepperoni sausage, sliced
1 small or ½ large red onion, sliced
45ml/3 tbsp bottled pesto
150ml/ ¼ pint/ ⅔ cup double (heavy) cream
225g/8oz cherry tomatoes, halved
15g/½ oz fresh chives
salt
breadsticks, to serve

1 Bring a large pan of lightly salted water to the boil and cook the pasta until it is *al dente*.

2 Meanwhile, heat the pepperoni sausage slices in a heavy frying pan over a medium-low heat until the fat runs. Add the sliced onion and cook, stirring occasionally, until it is softened and translucent.

3 Mix the pesto sauce and cream together in a small bowl. Add this mixture to the frying pan and stir over a low heat until the sauce is smooth.

4 Add the cherry tomatoes to the pepperoni mixture and snip the chives over the top with scissors. Stir again.

5 Drain the pasta and return it to the clean pan. Pour the sauce over and toss thoroughly, making sure all the pasta is coated. Serve immediately with breadsticks.

Cook's Tips

- *Use a mixture of red and yellow cherry tomatoes for a really colourful meal.*
- *You can use any fairly firm spicy cooking sausage for this recipe. Try mild or hot chorizo, or even black pudding.*

Rigatoni with Spicy Sausage & Tomato Sauce

This is really a cheat's version of Bolognese sauce, using the wonderful fresh spicy sausages sold in every Italian delicatessen.

Serves 4

450g/1lb fresh spicy Italian cooking sausage
30ml/2 tbsp olive oil
1 medium onion, chopped
450ml/ ¾ pint/1¾ cups passata (bottled strained tomatoes)
150ml/ ¼ pint/ ⅔ cup dry red wine
6 sun-dried tomatoes in oil, drained and sliced
450g/1lb/4 cups dried rigatoni
salt and freshly ground black pepper
chopped mixed fresh herbs, to garnish
freshly grated Parmesan cheese, to serve

1 Squeeze the sausages out of their skins. Put them in a bowl and break up the meat.

2 Heat the oil in a heavy pan. Add the onion and fry over a medium heat, stirring occasionally, for 5 minutes, until soft and golden. Stir in the sausagemeat and cook, browning it all over and breaking up the lumps with a wooden spoon.

3 Pour in the passata and the wine, and bring to the boil. Add the sun-dried tomatoes and season with salt and pepper to taste. Lower the heat and simmer for 10–12 minutes, or for as long as it takes to cook the pasta.

4 Bring a pan of lightly salted water to the boil and cook the pasta until *al dente*. Drain and divide among warmed bowls. Top with the sauce. Garnish with herbs and serve with Parmesan.

Cook's Tip

Passata is a concentrate of crushed, strained tomatoes, which has a deep, rich flavour.

Bamie Goreng

This fried noodle dish is wonderfully accommodating. You can add extra vegetables, or vary the meat content, depending on what you have to hand, bearing in mind the need to achieve a balance of colours, flavours and textures.

Serves 6–8

450g/1lb dried egg noodles
2 eggs, beaten
90ml/6 tbsp vegetable oil
25g/1oz/2 tbsp butter
2 garlic cloves, crushed
1 skinless, boneless chicken breast portion, thinly sliced
115g/4oz pork fillet (tenderloin), thinly sliced
115g/4oz calf's liver, trimmed and thinly sliced
115g/4oz/1 cup cooked peeled prawns (shrimp)
115g/4oz Chinese leaves (Chinese cabbage)
2 celery sticks, thinly sliced
4 spring onions (scallions), shredded
about 60ml/4 tbsp chicken stock
soy sauce
salt and freshly ground black pepper
deep-fried onions and fresh celery leaves, to garnish

1 Bring a large pan of lightly salted water to the boil and cook the noodles for 3–4 minutes. Drain, rinse under cold water and drain again. Set aside.

2 Season the eggs with salt and pepper to taste. Heat 5ml/1 tsp of the oil with the butter in a small pan. When the butter has melted, add the eggs and stir over a medium heat until lightly scrambled. Set aside.

3 Preheat a wok and add the remaining vegetable oil. When hot, stir-fry the garlic with the chicken, pork and liver over a medium-high heat for 2–3 minutes, until they have changed colour. Add the prawns, Chinese leaves, celery and spring onions and toss well.

4 Add the noodles to the wok and toss over the heat until heated through. Moisten with a little stock and flavour with soy sauce to taste. Finally, stir in the scrambled eggs. Garnish with deep-fried onions and celery leaves. Serve immediately.

Special Fried Noodles

This tasty dish from Singapore has much in common with the famous Indonesian Bamie Goreng, but tends to be spicier.

Serves 4–6

275g/10oz dried egg noodles
1 skinless, boneless chicken breast portion
115g/4oz lean pork
30ml/2 tbsp vegetable oil
175g/6oz/1½ cups cooked peeled prawns (shrimp)
4 shallots, chopped
2cm/¾in piece of fresh root ginger, peeled and thinly sliced
2 garlic cloves, crushed
45ml/3 tbsp light soy sauce
5–10ml/1–2 tsp chilli sauce
15ml/1 tbsp rice vinegar
5ml/1 tsp granulated sugar
2.5ml/½ tsp salt
225g/8oz fresh spinach leaves, shredded
3 spring onions (scallions), shredded

1 Bring a large pan of lightly salted water to the boil and cook the noodles for 3–4 minutes. Drain, rinse under cold water and drain again. Set aside.

2 Slice the chicken and pork thinly against the grain. Preheat a large wok. Add the vegetable oil. When hot, add the chicken, pork and prawns and stir-fry for 2–3 minutes. Add the shallots, ginger and garlic, and stir-fry without letting them colour.

3 Add the soy sauce, chilli sauce, vinegar, sugar and salt. Bring to a simmer, add the spinach and spring onions, cover and steam for 3–4 minutes.

4 Add the noodles and toss over the heat until they are hot and all the ingredients are well mixed. Serve immediately.

Cook's Tips
- *Put the chicken breast portion and pork in the freezer for 30 minutes before slicing to firm the meat.*
- *The prawns (shrimp) look more attractive if the heads and shells are removed but the tails are left intact.*

Tossed Noodles with Seafood

Surprisingly substantial, this is a very good way of serving seafood.

Serves 4–6

350g/12oz thick dried egg noodles
225g/8oz mussels, scrubbed and bearded
60ml/4 tbsp vegetable oil
3 slices of fresh root ginger, grated
2 garlic cloves, finely chopped
225g/8oz raw prawns (shrimp), peeled and deveined
225g/8oz prepared squid, cut into rings
115g/4oz Asian fried fish cake, sliced
1 red (bell) pepper, seeded and cut into rings
50g/2oz/ ⅓ cup sugar snap peas, trimmed
30ml/2 tbsp soy sauce
2.5ml/ ½ tsp sugar
120ml/4fl oz/ ½ cup fish stock
15ml/1 tbsp cornflour (cornstarch)
5–10ml/1–2 tsp sesame oil
salt and freshly ground black pepper
chopped spring onions (scallions) and fresh red chillies, to garnish

1 Bring a large pan of lightly salted water to the boil and cook the noodles until just tender. Drain and set aside.

2 Check the mussels and discard any that are not tightly closed, or which fail to shut when tapped with the back of a knife.

3 Heat a wok until hot, add the oil and swirl it around. Stir-fry the ginger and garlic for 30 seconds. Add the mussels, prawns and squid, put a lid on the wok and steam the seafood for about 4–5 minutes, until the prawns have changed colour and the mussel shells have opened. Discard any mussels that remain shut. Add the fish cake slices, red pepper rings and sugar snap peas and stir well.

4 In a bowl, mix the soy sauce, sugar, stock and cornflour. Stir into the shellfish and bring to the boil. Add the noodles and cook until they are heated through.

5 Add the sesame oil to the noodle mixture and season with salt and pepper to taste. Serve immediately, garnished with the spring onions and red chillies.

Seafood Chow Mein

Chow Mein originated in North America and is based on a traditional Chinese dish. It tastes delicious.

Serves 4

75g/3oz prepared squid
75g/3oz raw prawns (shrimp), peeled and deveined
3–4 shelled fresh scallops
½ egg white
15ml/1 tbsp cornflour (cornstarch) mixed to a paste with 30ml/2 tbsp water
250g/9oz dried egg noodles
75–90ml/5–6 tbsp vegetable oil
50g/2oz/ ⅓ cup mangetouts (snow peas)
2.5ml/ ½ tsp salt
2.5ml/ ½ tsp light brown sugar
15ml/1 tbsp Chinese rice wine or dry sherry
30ml/2 tbsp light soy sauce
2 spring onions (scallions), finely shredded, and a few drops of sesame oil, to garnish

1 Open up the squid and score the inside in a criss-cross pattern. Cut the squid into pieces, each about the size of a postage stamp. Soak these in a bowl of boiling water until all the pieces curl up. Drain, rinse in cold water and drain again.

2 Cut each prawn in half lengthways and cut each scallop into three slices. Whisk the egg white and cornflour paste in a bowl, add the scallops and prawns and toss them in the mixture.

3 Bring a large pan of lightly salted water to the boil and cook the noodles until tender. Drain, rinse under cold water and drain again. Put into a bowl and mix with about 15ml/1 tbsp of the vegetable oil.

4 Heat a wok and add 30–45ml/2–3 tbsp of the oil. When it is hot, stir-fry the mangetouts and seafood for 2 minutes. Add the salt, sugar, wine or sherry and half of the soy sauce and toss over the heat for 1 minute, then remove and keep warm.

5 Heat the remaining oil in the wok and stir-fry the noodles for 2–3 minutes with the remaining soy sauce. Place in a large serving dish, pour the shellfish mixture on top, garnish with the spring onions and sprinkle with the sesame oil.

Fried Cellophane Noodles & Prawns

Cellophane noodles look like delicate strands of blown glass in this stir-fry.

Serves 4

175g/6oz dried cellophane noodles
45ml/3 tbsp vegetable oil
3 garlic cloves, finely chopped
115g/4oz/1 cup cooked peeled prawns (shrimp)
2 lap cheong, rinsed, drained and finely diced
2 eggs
2 celery sticks, including leaves, diced
115g/4oz/2 cups beansprouts
115g/4oz spinach, cut into large pieces
2 spring onions (scallions), chopped
15–30ml/1–2 tbsp fish sauce
5ml/1 tsp sesame oil
15ml/1 tbsp toasted sesame seeds, to garnish

1 Soak the cellophane noodles in a bowl of hot water for about 10 minutes, or until soft. Drain the noodles and cut them into 10cm/4in lengths.

2 Heat a wok until hot, add the oil and swirl it around. Stir-fry the garlic until golden brown. Add the prawns and lap cheong and stir-fry for 2–3 minutes. Stir in the noodles and stir-fry for 2 minutes more.

3 Make a well in the centre of the prawn mixture, break in the eggs and slowly stir them until they are creamy and just set.

4 Stir in the celery, beansprouts, spinach and spring onions. Season with fish sauce and stir in the sesame oil. Continue to stir-fry until all the ingredients are cooked, mixing well. Transfer to a warmed serving dish. Garnish with the sesame seeds and serve immediately.

Cook's Tip
Lap cheong are Chinese wind-dried sausages. Sold in pairs, tied together with string, they are available from Chinese and Asian supermarkets.

Thai Fried Noodles

This tasty dish, made with rice noodles, is one of the national dishes of Thailand.

Serves 4–6

45ml/3 tbsp vegetable oil
15ml/1 tbsp chopped garlic
16 raw king prawns (jumbo shrimp), peeled, tails left intact and deveined
2 eggs, lightly beaten
15ml/1 tbsp dried shrimp, rinsed
30ml/2 tbsp pickled white radish
50g/2oz fried beancurd (tofu), cut into small slivers
2.5ml/ ½ tsp dried chilli flakes
350g/12oz rice noodles, soaked in warm water until soft
115g/4oz garlic chives, chopped
225g/8oz/4 cups beansprouts
50g/2oz/ ½ cup roasted peanuts, coarsely ground
5ml/1 tsp sugar
15ml/1 tbsp dark soy sauce
30ml/2 tbsp fish sauce
30ml/2 tbsp tamarind juice
fresh coriander (cilantro) leaves and kaffir lime wedges, to garnish

1 Heat a wok until hot, add 15ml/1 tbsp of the oil and swirl it around. Sir-fry the garlic until golden. Stir in the prawns and cook for 1–2 minutes until pink, tossing from time to time. Remove and set aside.

2 Heat another 15ml/1 tbsp of oil in the wok. Add the eggs and scramble them lightly. Remove from the wok and set aside.

3 Heat the remaining oil in the wok. Add the dried shrimp, pickled radish, beancurd and dried chilli flakes. Stir-fry briefly. Drain the rice noodles thoroughly, add them to the wok and stir-fry for 5 minutes.

4 Add the garlic chives with half the beansprouts and half the peanuts. Season with the sugar, soy sauce, fish sauce and tamarind juice. Mix well and cook, stirring frequently, until the noodles are heated through.

5 Return the prawns and eggs to the wok and mix with the noodles, tossing the mixture together. Garnish with the rest of the beansprouts and peanuts, the coriander leaves and the lime wedges. Serve immediately.

MIDWEEK MEALS

It's been a busy day at work or looking after the children – or both – and, once again, the family is hungry and supper time has come around. What could be tastier and easier, more nourishing and economical than pasta? Even children – often such fussy eaters – will relish Simple Baked Lasagne or Tagliatelle with Bolognese Sauce. This chapter features recipes for substantial baked dishes – just the thing for a cold winter evening – as well as speedier pasta sauces that are tasty and nourishing. The versatility of pasta makes it the perfect choice for family suppers. You will find a dish here to suit all tastes with mouth-watering sauces based on fish, chicken, tomatoes, mushrooms, cheese, bacon, beef, sausages, salami and an array of fresh vegetables. Midweek entertaining is easy, too, with delectable dishes, such as Tagliatelle with Avocado & Haddock Sauce or Pappardelle with Chicken & Mushrooms, that are ideal for an informal supper party. There are recipes for every kind of cook – dishes that need time to marinate for those who are well organized and like to plan their menus in advance, as well as simple, pantry sauces for last-minute decision makers. From tried and tested favourites to contemporary and imaginative innovations, rich and creamy to piquant and spicy and light and refreshing to warming and satisfying, pasta makes a super supper.

Rigatoni with Tomato & Tuna Sauce

Ridged pasta tubes trap the delectable sauce.

Serves 4

30ml/2 tbsp olive oil
1 onion, chopped
2 garlic cloves, chopped
400g/14oz can chopped tomatoes
60ml/4 tbsp tomato purée (paste)
350g/12oz dried rigatoni
50g/2oz/ ½ cup pitted black olives, quartered
5ml/1 tsp dried fresh oregano
225g/8oz can tuna in oil, drained and flaked
2.5ml/ ½ tsp anchovy purée
15ml/1 tbsp bottled capers, rinsed and drained
115g/4oz/1 cup grated Cheddar cheese
45ml/3 tbsp fresh white breadcrumbs
salt and freshly ground black pepper
fresh flat leaf parsley sprigs, to garnish

1 Heat the oil in a frying pan and fry the onion and garlic for about 10 minutes, until softened. Stir in the tomatoes and tomato purée, with salt and pepper to taste. Bring to the boil, then simmer gently for 10–15 minutes, stirring occasionally.

2 Meanwhile, bring a large pan of lightly salted water to the boil. Add the pasta and cook until *al dente.*

3 Stir the olives, oregano, tuna, anchovy purée and capers into the tomato sauce. Heat through for 2 minutes, then spoon the mixture into a bowl. Drain the pasta, toss it with the sauce, then divide it among four heatproof serving bowls.

4 Combine the cheese and breadcrumbs and sprinkle a quarter of the mixture over each portion. Place under a hot grill (broiler) until the cheese has melted. Serve immediately, garnished with the flat leaf parsley.

Cook's Tip
This speedy sauce is perfect for impromptu suppers, because most of the ingredients are store-cupboard (pantry) items.

Tagliatelle with Avocado & Haddock Sauce

Start making this dish the day before you plan to serve it, as the haddock needs to marinate overnight.

Serves 4

2.5ml/ ½ tsp each ground cumin, ground coriander and ground turmeric
150ml/ ¼ pint/ ⅔ cup fromage frais or cream cheese
150ml/ ¼ pint/ ⅔ cup double (heavy) cream
15ml/1 tbsp lemon juice
350g/12oz fresh haddock fillets, skinned and cut into bitesize chunks
25g/1oz/2 tbsp butter
1 onion, chopped
15ml/1 tbsp plain (all-purpose) flour
150ml/ ¼ pint/ ⅔ cup fish stock
350g/12oz fresh tagliatelle
1 avocado, peeled, stoned (pitted) and sliced
2 tomatoes, seeded and chopped
salt and freshly ground black pepper
fresh rosemary sprigs, to garnish

1 Mix the cumin, coriander, turmeric, fromage frais or cream cheese, cream and lemon juice in a bowl. Add a little salt and pepper, then stir in the haddock until all the chunks are coated. Cover and marinate in the refrigerator overnight.

2 Heat the butter in a frying pan and fry the onion over a low heat for about 10 minutes, until softened. Stir in the flour, then blend in the stock until smooth. Carefully stir in the haddock mixture. Cook over a medium heat, stirring frequently, until the haddock is cooked.

3 Meanwhile, bring a pan of lightly salted water to the boil, add the pasta and cook until it is *al dente*.

4 Gently stir the avocado slices and chopped tomatoes into the haddock mixture. Drain the pasta and return it to the pan. Pour over the sauce and toss gently to mix. Divide among four serving plates, garnish with the fresh rosemary and serve.

Cannelloni Sorrentina-style

Anchovies add zing to the filling in these pasta rolls.

Serves 4–6

60ml/4 tbsp olive oil
1 small onion, finely chopped
900g/2lb ripe tomatoes, peeled and finely chopped
2 garlic cloves, crushed
1 large handful fresh basil leaves, shredded, plus extra basil leaves, to garnish
250ml/8fl oz/1 cup vegetable stock
250ml/8fl oz/1 cup dry white wine
30ml/2 tbsp sun-dried tomato purée (paste)
2.5ml/ ½ tsp granulated sugar
16–18 fresh or dried lasagne sheets
250g/9oz/1 ⅓ cups ricotta cheese
130g/4½ oz packet mozzarella cheese, drained and diced small
8–9 drained canned anchovy fillets in olive oil, halved lengthways
50g/2oz/ ⅔ cup freshly grated Parmesan cheese
salt and freshly ground black pepper

1 Heat the oil in a pan and fry the onion gently until softened. Stir in the tomatoes, garlic and half the basil. Season, then toss over a medium heat for 5 minutes.

2 Scoop half the mixture into a bowl and set aside to cool. Stir the stock, wine, tomato purée and sugar into the remaining mixture and simmer for about 20 minutes, stirring occasionally.

3 Meanwhile, cook the lasagne sheets according to the instructions on the packet. Drain and lay flat on a dishtowel.

4 Preheat the oven to 190°C/375°F/Gas 5. Add the ricotta and mozzarella to the bowl. Stir in the remaining basil and season. Spread a little of the mixture over each lasagne sheet. Top with anchovy, then roll up like a Swiss (jelly) roll.

5 Process the tomato sauce in a food processor to a purée. Spread one-third over the base of an ovenproof dish. Arrange the cannelloni seam side down and spoon the remaining sauce over them. Sprinkle the Parmesan over the top and bake for 20 minutes. Serve hot, garnished with the extra basil leaves.

Cannelloni with Tuna

Everyone loves this pasta dish and it's a particular favourite with children. Italian Fontina cheese has a sweet, nutty flavour and melts beautifully.

Serves 4–6

50g/2oz/ ¼ cup butter
50g/2oz/ ½ cup plain (all-purpose) flour
about 900ml/1 ½ pints/3¾ cups hot milk
2 x 200g/7oz cans tuna, drained
115g/4oz/1 cup grated Fontina cheese
1.5 ml/ ¼ tsp freshly grated nutmeg
12 no-precook cannelloni tubes
50g2oz/ ⅔ cup freshly grated Parmesan cheese
salt and freshly ground black pepper
fresh herbs, to garnish

1 Melt the butter in a heavy pan, add the flour and cook over a low heat, stirring constantly, for 1–2 minutes. Gradually add 350ml/12fl oz/1 ½ cups of the milk, stirring constantly until the sauce boils and thickens. Remove the pan from the heat.

2 Transfer 120ml/4fl oz/ ½ cup of the warm white sauce to a bowl. Flake the tuna and stir it into the sauce in the bowl. Season with salt and pepper to taste. Preheat the oven to 180°C/350°F/Gas 4.

3 Return the pan containing the rest of the sauce to the heat, gradually whisk in the remaining milk, then add the grated Fontina and nutmeg and season with salt and pepper to taste. Simmer over a low heat, stirring constantly, for a few minutes, until the cheese has melted and the sauce is smooth.

4 Pour about one-third of the sauce into an ovenproof dish and spread to the corners.

5 Fill the cannelloni tubes with the tuna mixture. Place them in a single layer in the dish. Pour over the remaining cheese sauce and sprinkle with grated Parmesan. Bake for 30 minutes, or until the top is golden and bubbling. Serve immediately, garnished with the fresh herbs.

Conchiglie with Chicken Livers & Herbs

Fresh herbs and chicken livers are a good combination. Tossed with pasta shells, they make a very tasty supper dish.

Serves 4

50g/2oz/ ¼ cup butter
115g/4oz pancetta or rindless streaky (fatty) bacon, diced
250g/9oz frozen chicken livers, thawed, drained and diced
2 garlic cloves, crushed
10ml/2 tsp chopped fresh sage
300g/11oz/2¾ cups dried conchiglie
150ml/ ¼ pint/ ⅔ cup dry white wine
4 ripe tomatoes, peeled and diced
15ml/1 tbsp chopped fresh parsley
salt and freshly ground black pepper

1 Melt half the butter in a pan, add the pancetta or bacon and fry over a medium heat for a few minutes until it is lightly coloured, but not crisp.

2 Add the diced chicken livers, garlic and half the sage and season with plenty of pepper. Increase the heat and toss the livers for about 5 minutes, until they change colour all over.

3 Meanwhile, bring a large pan of lightly salted water to the boil and cook the pasta until it is *al dente*.

4 Pour the white wine over the chicken livers in the pan and let it sizzle for a few moments, then lower the heat and simmer gently for 5 minutes.

5 Add the remaining butter to the pan. As soon as it has melted, add the diced tomatoes, toss to mix, then add the remaining sage and the parsley. Stir thoroughly. Taste and add salt if needed.

6 Drain the pasta and tip it into a warmed serving bowl. Pour the chicken liver and herb sauce over and toss well to mix. Serve immediately.

Tagliatelle with Aubergines & Chicken Livers

Aubergines in a rich tomato sauce go very well with chicken livers. If cooking for vegetarian guests, use black olives instead.

Serves 4

675g/1½ lb dried tagliatelle
275g/10oz frozen chicken livers, thawed and drained
chopped flat leaf parsley, to garnish

For the sauce

2 large aubergines (eggplants), about 350g/12oz each
2 garlic cloves
1 large onion
90–120ml/6–8 tbsp oil
500ml/17fl oz/1¾ cups passata (bottled strained tomatoes)
250ml/8fl oz/1 cup boiling water
salt and freshly ground black pepper

1 To make the tomato sauce, peel the aubergines and dice the flesh. Place in a colander. Sprinkle with salt and leave to drain in the sink for 30 minutes. Rinse thoroughly under cold running water and squeeze dry. Crush the garlic and chop the onion.

2 Heat half the oil in a frying pan and sauté the onion for about 1 minute. Add the garlic and cook until the onion starts to brown. Using a slotted spoon, transfer the onion mixture to a plate. Brown the aubergine in the remaining oil.

3 Return the onion mixture to the pan and add the passata, boiling water and seasoning. Simmer for 30 minutes.

4 Preheat the grill (broiler). Bring a large pan of lightly salted water to the boil and cook the tagliatelle until it is *al dente*.

5 Meanwhile, place the chicken livers on oiled foil and grill (broil) for 3–4 minutes on each side. Snip into strips.

6 Drain the tagliatelle and place on warmed individual plates. Top each portion with the aubergine sauce and chicken livers. Garnish with the chopped flat leaf parsley.

Broccoli & Chicken Lasagne

A great example of how vegetables can add flavour and texture to a favourite dish and make it possible to use less meat.

Serves 6

25g/1oz/2 tbsp butter, plus extra for greasing
450g/1lb broccoli, broken into florets
15ml/1 tbsp sunflower oil
450g/1lb skinless, boneless chicken breast portions, cut into thin strips
1 onion, finely chopped
1 garlic clove, chopped
600ml/1 pint/2½ cups passata (bottled strained tomatoes)
2.5ml/½ tsp dried thyme
2.5ml/ ½ tsp dried oregano
12 sheets no-precook lasagne
275g/10oz/1¼ cups fromage frais or cream cheese
75g/3oz/1 cup freshly grated Parmesan cheese, plus extra for sprinkling
225g/8oz mozzarella cheese, thinly sliced
salt and freshly ground black pepper

1 Preheat the oven to 180°C/350°F/Gas 4 and grease a large shallow ovenproof dish with butter. Steam or boil the broccoli until nearly tender. Drain and set aside.

2 Heat the oil and butter in a frying pan and fry the chicken until lightly browned. Using a slotted spoon, transfer to a plate and set aside.

3 Add the onion and garlic to the pan and fry for 3–4 minutes. Stir in the passata and herbs and season with salt and pepper to taste. Cook, stirring frequently, for about 3–4 minutes, until the sauce has thickened slightly.

4 Spoon half the tomato sauce into the dish. Add four lasagne sheets, then half the chicken and half the broccoli. Dot with half the fromage frais or cream cheese and add half the Parmesan. Repeat the layers and top with the remaining lasagne.

5 Arrange the mozzarella cheese slices on top and sprinkle with the extra Parmesan. Bake for 30–35 minutes, until the top is golden. Leave to stand for 5 minutes before serving.

Farfalle with Chicken & Sausage

Just the thing for a midweek supper, this has a tasty, piquant flavour, thanks largely to the Italian sausage and sun-dried tomatoes.

Serves 4

45ml/3 tbsp olive oil
450g/1lb skinless, boneless chicken breast portions, cubed
3 Italian sausages, cut diagonally in 5mm/ ¼in slices
6 spring onions (scallions), sliced
10 drained sun-dried tomatoes in oil, chopped
250ml/8fl oz/1 cup passata (bottled strained tomatoes)
350g/12oz/3 cups dried farfalle
1 courgette (zucchini), cut diagonally in 5mm/ ¼in slices
salt and freshly ground black pepper

1 Heat the olive oil in a large, heavy frying pan. Add the chicken and sausage slices, with a little salt and pepper, and cook for about 10 minutes, until browned. With a slotted spoon, remove the chicken and sausage pieces from the pan, and drain on kitchen paper.

2 Add the spring onions and sun-dried tomato pieces to the pan and cook for 5 minutes, then stir in the passata. Cook the sauce for about 10 minutes, stirring occasionally, until it is thick and flavoursome.

3 Meanwhile, bring a large pan of lightly salted water to the boil and cook the pasta until it is *al dente*.

4 Add the courgette to the tomato sauce, with the chicken and sausage slices. Cook for 5 minutes.

5 Drain the pasta, return it to the clean pan and toss with the sauce. Serve immediately in heated bowls.

Cook's Tip
A wide variety of Italian cooking sausages – salsiccia *– is available from good delicatessens.*

Farfalle with Chicken & Cherry Tomatoes

Quick to prepare and easy to cook, this colourful dish is full of flavour.

Serves 4

350g/12oz skinless, boneless chicken breast portions, cut into bitesize pieces
60ml/4 tbsp dry vermouth
10ml/2 tsp chopped fresh rosemary
15ml/1 tbsp olive oil
1 onion, finely chopped
90g/3½ oz piece Italian salami, diced
275g/10oz/2½ cups dried farfalle
15ml/1 tbsp balsamic vinegar
400g/14oz can Italian cherry tomatoes
good pinch of crushed dried red chillies
salt and freshly ground black pepper
4 fresh rosemary sprigs, to garnish

1 Put the chicken in a bowl, pour in the vermouth and sprinkle with half the rosemary. Season to taste, stir well and set aside.

2 Heat the oil in a pan and fry the onion and salami for 5 minutes, stirring frequently. Bring a large pan of lightly salted water to the boil and cook the pasta until it is *al dente*.

3 Add the chicken and vermouth to the onion and salami, increase the heat to high and fry for 3 minutes, or until the chicken is white all over. Sprinkle the vinegar over the chicken. Add the cherry tomatoes and dried chillies. Stir well and simmer for a few minutes more. Taste the sauce for seasoning.

4 Drain the pasta and return it to the clean pan. Add the sauce and remaining chopped rosemary and toss well. Serve in warmed bowls, garnished with the rosemary sprigs.

Cook's Tip
If you like, you can crush the tomatoes with the back of a wooden spoon while they are simmering in the pan.

Pappardelle with Chicken & Mushrooms

Rich and creamy, this is a good supper party dish.

Serves 4

15g/½oz/¼ cup dried porcini mushrooms
175ml/6fl oz/¾ cup warm water
25g/1oz/2 tbsp butter
1 garlic clove, crushed
1 small handful fresh parsley, coarsely chopped
1 small leek, chopped
120ml/4fl oz/½ cup dry white wine
250ml/8fl oz/1 cup chicken stock
400g/14oz fresh or dried pappardelle
2 skinless, boneless chicken breast portions, cut into thin strips
105ml/7 tbsp mascarpone cheese
salt and freshly ground black pepper
fresh basil leaves, shredded, to garnish

1 Put the mushrooms in a bowl. Pour over the warm water. Leave to soak for 15–20 minutes, then tip into a fine sieve set over a large pan and squeeze the mushrooms with your hands to release as much liquid as possible. Chop the mushrooms finely and set them aside. Reserve the strained soaking liquid.

2 Melt the butter in a wide, shallow pan and add the mushrooms, garlic, parsley and leek, with salt and pepper to taste. Cook over a low heat, stirring frequently, for 5 minutes, then pour in the wine and stock and bring to the boil. Lower the heat and simmer for about 5 minutes, or until the liquid has reduced and is thickened.

3 Add plenty of lightly salted water to the strained soaking liquid, bring to the boil and cook the pasta until *al dente*.

4 Add the chicken to the sauce and simmer for 5 minutes, or until just tender. Add the mascarpone, a spoonful at a time, stirring well after each addition, then add one to two spoonfuls of the water used for cooking the pasta. Taste for seasoning.

5 Drain the pasta and tip it into a large bowl. Add the chicken and sauce and toss well. Serve, topped with the shredded basil.

Turkey, Mushroom & Pasta Bake

This is an excellent recipe for using up leftover roast turkey. Baking the pasta gives you time to make an accompanying salad.

Serves 4

65g/2½oz/5 tbsp butter, plus extra for greasing
225g/8oz/3 cups mushrooms, thinly sliced
25g/1oz/¼ cup plain (all-purpose) flour
400ml/14fl oz/1⅔ cups milk
450ml/¾ pint/1¾ cups chicken stock
60ml/4 tbsp dry white wine
275g/10oz dried spaghetti
350g/12oz cooked turkey, chopped
115g/4oz/1 cup frozen peas, thawed
75g/3oz/1 cup freshly grated Parmesan cheese
25g/1oz/½ cup fresh white breadcrumbs
salt and freshly ground black pepper
green salad, to serve

1 Preheat the oven to 190°C/375°F/Gas 5. Grease a 3 litre/5 pint/6 cup ovenproof dish.

2 Melt 50g/2oz/4 tbsp of the butter in a pan. Cook the mushrooms for 5 minutes, stirring frequently. Stir in the flour and cook for 3 minutes, stirring constantly. Gradually add the milk, stock and white wine, stirring constantly until the sauce boils and thickens. Lower the heat and simmer for 5 minutes.

3 Meanwhile, bring a large pan of lightly salted water to the boil and cook the pasta until it is *al dente*. Drain the pasta and put it in a mixing bowl.

4 Pour in the mushroom sauce and mix well. Stir in the turkey, peas and half the Parmesan, and season with salt and pepper to taste. Transfer the mixture to the prepared dish.

5 In a small bowl, combine the remaining Parmesan with the breadcrumbs. Sprinkle evenly over the turkey mixture. Dot with the remaining butter, cut into pieces. Bake for 30–40 minutes, until bubbling and golden. Serve with a green salad.

Spaghetti Tetrazzini

This American-Italian recipe makes a rich and filling family meal.

Serves 4–6

75g/3oz/6 tbsp butter
350g/12oz turkey breast fillet, cut into thin strips
2 pieces drained bottled roasted (bell) pepper, rinsed, dried and cut into thin strips
175g/6oz dried spaghetti
50g/2oz/½ cup plain (all-purpose) flour
900ml/1½ pints/3¾ cups hot milk
115g/4oz/1⅓ cups freshly grated Parmesan cheese
1.5–2.5ml/¼–½ tsp dried English (hot) mustard
salt and freshly ground black pepper
salad leaves, to garnish

1 Melt about one-third of the butter in a pan, add the turkey, and sprinkle with a little salt and plenty of pepper. Toss the turkey over a medium heat for about 5 minutes, until the meat turns white, then add the roasted pepper strips and toss to mix. Remove with a slotted spoon and set aside.

2 Preheat the oven to 180°C/350°F/Gas 4. Bring a large pan of lightly salted water to the boil and cook the pasta until *al dente*.

3 Meanwhile, melt the remaining butter in the pan in which the turkey was cooked. Add the flour and cook, stirring constantly, for 1 minute. Gradually add the hot milk, stirring constantly until the sauce boils and thickens.

4 Add two-thirds of the grated Parmesan to the white sauce, then whisk in mustard, with salt and pepper to taste. Remove the sauce from the heat.

5 Drain the pasta and return it to the clean pan. Mix in half the cheese sauce, then spoon the mixture around the edge of an ovenproof dish. Stir the turkey mixture into the remaining cheese sauce and spoon into the centre of the dish.

6 Sprinkle the remaining Parmesan over the top and bake for 15–20 minutes until the topping is crisp. Serve with salad leaves.

Spätzle

This simple pasta dish comes from Germany, where it is served with many savoury dishes. It goes particularly well with poached celery hearts.

Serves 4

350g/12oz/3 cups plain (all-purpose) flour
2 eggs, beaten
about 200ml/7fl oz/scant 1 cup milk and water combined
15ml/1 tbsp sunflower oil
25g/1oz/2 tbsp butter
4 rindless streaky (fatty) bacon rashers (strips), diced
salt and freshly ground black pepper

1 Sift the flour and 2.5ml/½ tsp salt into a bowl and make a well in the centre. Add the eggs and enough of the milk and water to make a very soft dough. Beat the dough until it develops bubbles, then stir in the oil and beat again. Bring a large pan of lightly salted water to the boil.

2 Dampen a chopping board with water and place the dough on it. Using the broad side of a knife, shave off strips of the dough, then gently push them off the board so that they fall into the boiling water. Do not overcrowd the pan. Cook the spätzle for 3 minutes, then lift them out with a slotted spoon and put them in a colander. Rinse quickly under hot water, put in a warmed serving bowl and cover to keep warm. Repeat until all the dough has been used up.

3 Melt the butter in a frying pan and fry the bacon until crisp. Pour the contents of the pan over the spätzle and season with black pepper. Serve immediately.

Cook's Tip

When shaving the dough, occasionally rinse the knife with water, so that the dough does not stick to it. The faster you work at this stage, the lighter the texture of the spätzle will be.

Spaghetti with Pancetta & Two-way Tomatoes

Sun-dried tomatoes add an extra dimension to a fresh tomato sauce in this simple spaghetti dish.

Serves 4

115g/4oz diced pancetta
15ml/1 tbsp olive oil
1 large onion, finely chopped
4 drained sun-dried tomatoes in oil, diced
2 beefsteak tomatoes, peeled and diced
350g/12oz dried spaghetti
leaves from 2–3 fresh marjoram sprigs
salt and freshly ground black pepper
thin shavings of Pecorino cheese, to serve

1 Put the pancetta in a heavy pan. Stir over a low heat until the fat runs. Add the oil. When it is hot, add the onion and sun-dried tomatoes and cook gently, stirring constantly, for about 10 minutes.

2 Stir in the fresh tomatoes and season with salt and pepper to taste. Cook for about 10 minutes, stirring occasionally.

3 Meanwhile, bring a large pan of lightly salted water to the boil. Add the pasta and cook until it is *al dente*. Drain and return to the clean pan.

4 Stir the marjoram into the sauce, then add it to the pasta and toss well. Serve immediately in warmed bowls, topped with the shavings of Pecorino.

Cook's Tips

- *Look for diced pancetta in packets in the chiller cabinet of your local supermarket. Some delicatessens sell it in slices cut from a roll, which you can dice yourself.*
- *For an even stronger tomato flavour, substitute the oil from the sun-dried tomatoes for the olive oil.*

Piquant Penne with Bacon & Chillies

This can be mildly spicy or fiercely fiery, depending on how much chilli you use.

Serves 4

25g/1oz/scant ½ cup dried porcini mushrooms
90g/3½ oz/7 tbsp butter
150g/5oz rindless smoked streaky (fatty) bacon, diced
1–2 dried red chillies, or to taste
2 garlic cloves, crushed
8 ripe plum tomatoes, peeled and chopped
a few fresh basil leaves, torn, plus extra to garnish
350g/12oz/3 cups fresh or dried penne
50g/2oz/ ⅔ cup freshly grated Parmesan cheese
25g/1oz/ ⅓ cup freshly grated Pecorino cheese
salt

1 Soak the dried mushrooms in warm water to cover for 15–20 minutes. Drain, then squeeze dry with your hands. Finely chop the mushrooms.

2 Melt 50g/2oz/4 tbsp of the butter in a pan and fry the bacon until slightly crisp. Remove it with a slotted spoon and set it aside. Add the chopped mushrooms to the pan, fry for about 2 minutes, then add to the bacon. Crumble one chilli into the fat remaining in the pan and cook the garlic until it is golden.

3 Add the tomatoes and basil, and season with salt. Cook gently, stirring occasionally, for 10–15 minutes. Meanwhile, bring a large pan of lightly salted water to the boil and cook the penne until *al dente*.

4 Add the bacon and mushrooms to the tomato sauce. Taste and add more chillies if you prefer a hotter flavour. If the sauce is too dry, stir in a little of the pasta water.

5 Drain the pasta and tip it into a warmed bowl. Dice the remaining butter, add it to the pasta with the cheeses, then toss until coated. Pour the tomato sauce over the pasta, toss well and serve immediately, with a few basil leaves sprinkled on top.

Pumpkin, Bacon & Parmesan Pasta

The sweetness of pumpkin is nicely balanced by the mature flavour of the Parmesan incorporated in the sauce.

Serves 4

800g/1¾ b fresh pumpkin flesh, cut into small cubes
300g/11oz dried tagliatelle
25g/1oz/2 tbsp butter
115g/4oz rindless smoked back (lean) bacon, diced
1 onion, sliced
150ml/ ¼ pint/ ⅔ cup single (light) cream
50g/2oz/ ⅔ cup freshly grated Parmesan cheese
freshly grated nutmeg
30ml/2 tbsp chopped fresh parsley
15ml/1 tbsp chopped fresh chives
salt and freshly ground black pepper
sprigs of fresh flat leaf parsley, to garnish
Garlic Breadcrumbs, to serve

1 Bring a large pan of lightly salted water to the boil. Tip in the pumpkin cubes. Cook over a medium heat for about 10 minutes, until just tender.

2 Using a slotted spoon, remove the pumpkin cubes from the water, put them in a bowl and keep them warm. Add the pasta to the boiling water in the pan and cook until *al dente*. Drain and set aside.

3 Heat the butter in the clean pasta pan and fry the bacon and onion for 5 minutes. Stir in the cream and bring to just below boiling point. Add the pasta and toss in the sauce until hot.

4 Stir in the pumpkin, Parmesan, nutmeg, chopped parsley and chives and season with salt and pepper to taste. Serve immediately, garnished with flat leaf parsley sprigs and sprinkled with the garlic breadcrumbs.

Cook's Tip

Pumpkins can grow to an enormous size – the record is about 180kg/400lb – and even more reasonable specimens, at about 3kg/6½lb, are still often too large for a single meal. Consequently, many supermarkets now sell pumpkin already cut into pieces. If buying this way, make sure that the flesh is firm, but not dried out or fibrous.

Garlic Breadcrumbs

These are beautifully crunchy and can be used to top any pasta dish.

Makes 75g/3oz/1½ cups

40g/1½ oz/3 tbsp butter
15ml/1 tbsp olive oil
2 garlic cloves, crushed
75g/3oz/1½ cups fresh white breadcrumbs

1 Melt the butter and oil in a frying pan. Add the garlic and breadcrumbs. Fry gently until the crumbs are golden brown and crisp. Drain on kitchen paper.

Three Tomato Bolognese

Although there's only one authentic Bolognese sauce, there are dozens of delicious dishes based on the famous ragoût. This one is well worth trying.

Serves 4–6

30ml/2 tbsp olive oil
1 onion, finely chopped
1 garlic clove, crushed
5ml/1 tsp dried mixed herbs
1.5ml/ ¼ tsp cayenne pepper
350–450g/12oz–1lb minced (ground) beef
400g/14oz can chopped tomatoes
45ml/3 tbsp tomato ketchup
15ml/1 tbsp sun-dried tomato purée (paste)
5ml/1 tsp Worcestershire sauce
5ml/1 tsp dried oregano
450ml/ ¾ pint/1¾ cups beef or vegetable stock
45ml/3 tbsp red wine
400–450g/14oz–1lb dried spaghetti
salt and freshly ground black pepper
freshly grated Parmesan cheese, to serve

1 Heat the olive oil in a large, heavy pan and fry the onion and garlic over a low heat, stirring frequently, for about 5 minutes, until softened. Stir in the mixed herbs and cayenne and cook for 2–3 minutes more.

2 Add the minced beef and cook gently for about 5 minutes, stirring frequently and breaking up any lumps in the meat with a wooden spoon.

3 Stir in the canned tomatoes, ketchup, sun-dried tomato purée, Worcestershire sauce, oregano and plenty of black pepper. Pour in the stock and red wine and bring to the boil, stirring. Cover the pan, lower the heat and simmer, stirring occasionally, for 30 minutes.

4 Bring a large pan of lightly salted water to the boil and cook the pasta until it is *al dente*. Drain and divide among warmed bowls. Taste the sauce and add salt if necessary, then spoon it on top of the pasta and sprinkle with a little grated Parmesan. Serve immediately, with extra Parmesan handed separately.

Tagliatelle with Meat Sauce

Using a combination of beef and pork with white wine and cream makes for a very rich, sophisticated sauce.

Serves 6–8

450g/1lb fresh or dried tagliatelle
freshly grated Parmesan cheese, to serve

For the meat sauce

25g/1oz/2 tbsp butter
15ml/1 tbsp olive oil
1 onion, finely chopped
2 carrots, finely chopped
2 celery sticks, finely chopped
2 garlic cloves, crushed
130g/4½oz pancetta or rindless streaky (fatty) bacon, diced
250g/9oz minced (ground) beef
250g/9oz minced (ground) pork
120ml/4fl oz/ ½ cup dry white wine
2 x 400g/14oz cans crushed Italian plum tomatoes
475–750ml/16fl oz–1¼ pints/ 2–3 cups beef stock
100ml/3½fl oz/scant ½ cup double (heavy) cream
salt and freshly ground black pepper

1 First, make the meat sauce. Heat the butter and oil in a large pan and cook the vegetables and the pancetta or bacon over a moderate heat, stirring frequently, for 10 minutes.

2 Add the minced beef and pork, lower the heat and cook gently for 10 minutes, stirring frequently and breaking up any lumps in the meat with a wooden spoon. Season to taste, then stir in the wine. Simmer for 5 minutes.

3 Add the canned tomatoes and 250ml/8fl oz/1 cup of the beef stock and bring to the boil. Stir the sauce well, then lower the heat. Partly cover the pan and simmer very gently for 2 hours. Stir occasionally and add more stock as it is absorbed.

4 Stir the cream into the sauce, then simmer, without a lid, for another 30 minutes, stirring frequently.

5 Bring a large pan of lightly salted water to the boil and cook the pasta until it is *al dente*. Drain it and tip it into a warmed bowl. Pour the sauce over the pasta and toss well. Serve, sprinkled with grated Parmesan.

Sardinian Sausage & Pasta

In Sardinia they call this dish "malloreddus", which is the local name for the type of pasta used to make it.

Serves 4–6

30ml/2 tbsp olive oil
6 garlic cloves
200g/7oz Italian pure pork sausage, diced small
2 small handfuls of fresh basil leaves
400g/14oz can chopped Italian plum tomatoes
a good pinch of saffron threads
15ml/1 tbsp granulated sugar
350g/12oz/3 cups dried malloreddus (gnocchi sardi) or other pasta shapes
75g/3oz/1 cup freshly grated Pecorino cheese
salt and freshly ground black pepper

1 Heat the oil in a pan and fry the garlic, sausage and half the basil leaves until the sausage is browned all over. Remove and discard the garlic.

2 Add the tomatoes. Fill the empty can with water; pour it into the pan, then stir in the saffron, sugar, 5ml/1 tsp salt and pepper to taste. Bring to the boil, lower the heat and simmer, stirring occasionally, for 20–30 minutes.

3 Meanwhile, bring a pan of lightly salted water to the boil and cook the pasta until it is *al dente*.

4 Drain the pasta and tip it into a warmed bowl. Pour the sauce over the pasta and toss well. Add about one-third of the Pecorino and the remaining basil and toss again. Serve immediately, with the remaining Pecorino sprinkled on top.

Cook's Tip
In Sardinia, a special type of sausage is used for malloreddus. *It is flavoured with aniseed and black pepper and is called* sartizzu sardo. *A good alternative would be the piquant* salsiccia piccante. *If, however, you like a slightly milder flavour, try* luganega, *which is much more widely available.*

Tortiglioni with Salami

Serve this heady pasta dish with a robust red wine.

Serves 4

30ml/2 tbsp olive oil
1 onion, finely chopped
1 celery stick, finely chopped
2 large garlic cloves, crushed
1 fresh red chilli, seeded and chopped
450g/1lb ripe plum tomatoes, peeled and finely chopped
30ml/2 tbsp tomato purée (paste)
150ml/ ¼ pint/ ⅔ cup red wine
5ml/1 tsp granulated sugar
300g/11oz/2¾ cups dried tortiglioni
175g/6oz spicy salami, rind removed, chopped into large chunks
salt and freshly ground black pepper
30ml/2 tbsp chopped fresh parsley, to garnish
freshly grated Parmesan cheese, to serve

1 Heat the oil in a large pan. Add the onion, celery, garlic and chilli and cook over a low heat, stirring frequently, for about 10 minutes, until softened.

2 Add the tomatoes, tomato purée, wine and sugar, and season with salt and pepper to taste. Bring to the boil, stirring constantly. Lower the heat, cover and simmer gently, stirring occasionally, for about 20 minutes. Add a few spoonfuls of water from time to time if the sauce becomes too thick.

3 Meanwhile, bring a large pan of lightly salted water to the boil and cook the pasta until it is *al dente*. Add the salami to the sauce and stir until heated through.

4 Drain the pasta, tip it into a large bowl, then pour the sauce over and toss to mix. Sprinkle over the parsley and serve with the grated Parmesan.

Cook's Tip
Buy the salami for this dish in a single piece so that you can chop it into large chunks.

Simple Baked Lasagne

This is a good basic lasagne for a family supper.

Serves 4

30ml/1 tbsp olive oil
1 onion, finely chopped
2 garlic cloves, chopped
1 celery stick, finely chopped
1 carrot, grated
450g/1lb minced (ground) beef
15–30ml/1–2 tbsp tomato purée (paste)
250–350ml/8–12fl oz/1–1½ cups vegetable stock
2 bay leaves
400g/14oz no-precook lasagne sheets
75g/3oz/1 cup freshly grated Parmesan cheese
15g/½ oz/1 tbsp butter

For the béchamel sauce

750ml/1¼ pints/3 cups milk
1 bay leaf
3 blades of mace
115g/4oz/½ cup butter
75g/3oz/¾ cup plain (all-purpose) flour
salt and freshly ground black pepper

1 Heat the oil in a large pan and fry the onion, garlic and celery until softened. Add the carrot and minced beef and cook for 10 minutes, then drain off the excess fat. Stir in the tomato purée and 250ml/8fl oz/1 cup of the stock. Add the bay leaves and cook over a low heat for 1–1½ hours, adding more stock as needed.

2 Make the béchamel sauce. Heat the milk in a pan, with the bay leaf and mace, to just below boiling point. Remove from the heat. Leave to infuse (steep) for 15 minutes, then scoop out the herbs. Melt the butter in a small pan and stir in the flour. Cook, stirring constantly, for 1 minute. Gradually add the milk, stirring until the sauce boils and thickens. Season to taste.

3 Preheat the oven to 200°C/400°/Gas 6. Spread a large spoonful of the meat sauce over the base of an ovenproof dish. Top with a layer of lasagne, cover with a thin layer of meat sauce, then a layer of béchamel sauce. Sprinkle with a little Parmesan. Repeat the layers, ending with a layer of pasta and béchamel. Sprinkle the rest of the Parmesan over and dot with the butter. Bake for 45 minutes. Leave to stand for 5–10 minutes before serving.

Three-cheese Lasagne

The cheese makes this lasagne quite expensive, so reserve this mouthwatering dish for a special occasion.

Serves 6–8

30ml/2 tbsp olive oil
1 onion, finely chopped
1 carrot, finely chopped
1 celery stick, finely chopped
1 garlic clove, crushed
675g/1½lb minced (ground) beef
400g/14oz can chopped tomatoes
300ml/½ pint/1¼ cups beef stock
300ml/½ pint/1¼ cups red wine
30ml/2 tbsp sun-dried tomato purée (paste)
10ml/2 tsp dried oregano
9 no-precook lasagne sheets
3 x 150g/5oz packets mozzarella cheese, thinly sliced
450g/1lb/2 cups ricotta cheese
115g/4oz/1⅓ cups freshly grated Parmesan cheese
salt and freshly ground black pepper

1 Heat the oil in a large pan. Add the onion, carrot, celery and garlic and cook over a low heat, stirring occasionally, for 10 minutes, until softened.

2 Add the minced beef and cook until it changes colour, stirring constantly and breaking it up with a wooden spoon. Drain off the excess fat.

3 Add the tomatoes, stock, wine, tomato purée and oregano and season with salt and pepper to taste. Bring to the boil, stirring constantly. Cover, lower the heat and simmer gently for 1 hour, stirring occasionally.

4 Preheat the oven to 190°C/375°F/Gas 5. Check for seasoning, then ladle one-third of the meat sauce into a 33 x 23cm/13 x 9in ovenproof dish and cover with three sheets of lasagne. Arrange one-third of the mozzarella slices over the top, dot with one-third of the ricotta, then sprinkle with one-third of the grated Parmesan.

5 Repeat these layers twice, then bake for 45 minutes, until golden brown and bubbling. Leave to stand for 10 minutes before serving.

Tagliatelle with Bolognese Sauce

Many people serve Bolognese sauce with spaghetti. To be absolutely correct, it should be served with tagliatelle.

Serves 4

30ml/2 tbsp olive oil
1 onion, finely chopped
1 carrot, finely chopped
1 celery stick, finely chopped
1 garlic clove, crushed
350g/12oz minced (ground) beef
150ml/ ¼ pint/ ⅔ cup red wine
250ml/8fl oz/1 cup milk
400g/14oz can chopped tomatoes
15ml/1 tbsp sun-dried tomato purée (paste)
350g/12oz fresh or dried tagliatelle
salt and freshly ground black pepper
shredded fresh basil, to garnish
grated Parmesan cheese, to serve

1 Heat the oil in a large pan and fry the onion, carrot, celery and garlic over a low heat for about 10 minutes, until softened. Stir frequently. Do not allow the vegetables to colour.

2 Add the beef and cook until it changes colour, breaking up any lumps with a wooden spoon. Pour in the wine. Stir frequently until it has evaporated, then add the milk and continue cooking and stirring until this has evaporated, too.

3 Stir in the tomatoes and tomato purée, with salt and pepper to taste. Simmer the sauce, uncovered, over the lowest possible heat for at least 45 minutes.

4 Bring a large pan of lightly salted water to the boil and cook the pasta until it is *al dente*. Drain and tip into a warmed large bowl. Pour over the sauce and toss to combine. Garnish with basil and serve, with Parmesan cheese handed separately.

Cook's Tip

Don't skimp on the cooking time – it is essential for a full-flavoured Bolognese sauce. Some Italian cooks insist on cooking it for 3–4 hours, so the longer the better.

Fettuccine Bolognese with Baby Tomatoes

This is a versatile meat sauce. You can toss it with freshly cooked pasta – the quantity here is enough for 450g/1lb tagliatelle, spaghetti or any short pasta shapes such as penne or fusilli – or alternatively you can layer it in a baked dish like lasagne.

Serves 4–6

45ml/3 tbsp olive oil
1 onion, finely chopped
1 small carrot, finely chopped
1 celery stick, finely chopped
2 garlic cloves, crushed
400g/14oz minced (ground) beef
120ml/4fl oz/ ½ cup red wine
200ml/7fl oz/scant 1 cup passata (bottled strained tomatoes)
15ml/1 tbsp tomato purée (paste)
5ml/1 tsp dried oregano
15ml/1 tbsp chopped fresh flat leaf parsley
about 350ml/12fl oz/1 ½ cups beef stock
8 baby Italian tomatoes
450g/1lb fresh fettuccine
salt and freshly ground black pepper
fresh Parmesan, to serve

1 Heat the oil in a large pan and cook the onion, carrot, celery and garlic over a low heat, stirring frequently, for 5–7 minutes.

2 Add the minced beef and cook for 5 minutes, stirring frequently and breaking up any lumps in the meat with a wooden spoon. Stir in the wine and mix well.

3 Cook for 1–2 minutes, then add the passata, tomato purée, oregano, parsley and 60ml/4 tbsp of the beef stock. Season with salt and pepper to taste. Stir well and bring to the boil over a moderate heat.

4 Lower the heat, cover the pan and simmer for 30 minutes, stirring from time to time and adding more stock as necessary. Add the tomatoes and simmer for 10 minutes more.

5 Bring a pan of lightly salted water to the boil and cook the fettuccine until *al dente*. Drain, return to the pan and add the sauce. Toss well, then serve with shavings of Parmesan.

Corsican Beef Stew with Macaroni

In Corsica, pasta is often served with gravy and, in this case, a rich beef stew.

Serves 4

25g/1oz/½ cup dried porcini mushrooms
6 garlic cloves
900g/2lb stewing beef, cut into 5cm/2in cubes
115g/4oz lardons, or rindless thick streaky (fatty) bacon cut into strips
45ml/3 tbsp olive oil
2 onions, sliced
300ml/ ½ pint/1 ¼ cups dry white wine
30ml/2 tbsp passata (bottled strained tomatoes)
pinch of ground cinnamon
fresh rosemary sprig
1 bay leaf
225g/8oz/2 cups large macaroni
50g/2oz/ ⅔ cup freshly grated Parmesan cheese
salt and freshly ground black pepper

1 Soak the mushrooms in warm water for 30 minutes. Drain, set them aside and reserve the liquid. Cut three garlic cloves into thin strips and insert them into the beef by making little slices with a sharp knife. Push the lardons or pieces of bacon into the beef with the garlic. Season the meat to taste.

2 Heat the oil in a heavy pan and brown the beef in batches. Transfer to a plate. Add the sliced onions to the pan and cook until lightly browned. Crush the remaining garlic and add to the onions. Return the meat to the pan. Stir in the white wine, passata, mushrooms, cinnamon, rosemary and bay leaf. Season with salt and pepper. Cook gently, stirring frequently, for 30 minutes.

3 Strain the mushroom liquid and add it to the stew with enough water to cover. Bring to the boil, cover and simmer very gently for 3 hours, until the meat is very tender.

4 Bring a large pan of lightly salted water to the boil and cook the macaroni until it is *al dente*. Lift the pieces of meat out of the gravy and transfer to a warmed serving platter. Drain the pasta and layer it in a serving bowl with the gravy and two-thirds of the cheese. Serve with the meat and the remaining cheese.

Pastitsio

Macaroni in a cheese sauce is layered with cinnamon and cumin-spiced minced beef to make a Greek version of lasagne.

Serves 4–6

225g/8oz/2 cups dried short-cut macaroni
30ml/2 tbsp olive oil
1 large onion, finely chopped
2 garlic cloves, crushed
450g/1lb minced (ground) steak
300ml/ ½ pint/1 ¼ cups beef stock
10ml/2 tsp tomato purée (paste)
5ml/1 tsp ground cinnamon
5ml/1 tsp ground cumin
15ml/1 tbsp chopped fresh mint
50g/2oz/ ¼ cup butter
40g/1 ½ oz/ ⅓ cup plain (all-purpose) flour
120ml/4fl oz/ ½ cup milk
120ml/4fl oz/ ½ cup natural (plain) yogurt
175g/6oz/1 ½ cups grated Kefalotiri cheese
salt and freshly ground black pepper

1 Bring a pan of lightly salted water to the boil and cook the macaroni until it is *al dente*. Drain, rinse under cold water and drain again. Set aside. Preheat the oven to 190°C/375°F/Gas 5.

2 Heat the oil in a frying pan. Add the onion and garlic and fry over a moderate heat, stirring frequently, for 5 minutes, until softened. Add the minced steak and stir until browned. Stir in the stock, tomato purée, cinnamon, cumin and mint and season with salt and pepper to taste. Cook gently for 10–15 minutes, until the sauce is thick and flavoursome.

3 Melt the butter in a pan. Stir in the flour and cook, stirring constantly, for 1 minute. Gradually add the milk and yogurt, stirring over a low heat until the sauce thickens. Stir in half the cheese and season with salt and pepper. Stir the macaroni into the cheese sauce.

4 Spread half the macaroni mixture over the bottom of a large ovenproof dish. Cover with the meat sauce and top with the remaining macaroni. Sprinkle the remaining cheese over the top and bake for 45 minutes or until golden brown on top.

Gingered Chicken Noodles

A blend of ginger, spices and coconut milk flavours this delicious supper dish, which is made in minutes.

Serves 4

350g/12oz skinless, boneless chicken breast portions
225g/8oz courgettes (zucchini)
275g/10oz aubergine (eggplant)
about 30ml/2 tbsp vegetable oil
5cm/2in piece of fresh root ginger, finely chopped
6 spring onions (scallions), sliced
10ml/2 tsp Thai green curry paste
400ml/14fl oz/1⅔ cups coconut milk
475ml/16fl oz/2 cups chicken stock
115g/4oz dried medium egg noodles
45ml/3 tbsp chopped fresh coriander (cilantro), plus extra, to garnish
15ml/1 tbsp lemon juice
salt and freshly ground black pepper

1 Cut the chicken into bitesize pieces. Halve the courgettes lengthways and roughly chop them. Cut the aubergine into pieces of a similar size.

2 Heat the oil in a large, shallow pan and stir-fry the chicken pieces until golden. Remove with a slotted spoon and drain on kitchen paper.

3 Add a little more oil to the pan, if necessary, and stir-fry the ginger and spring onions for 3 minutes. Add the courgettes and cook for 2–3 minutes, or until beginning to turn golden. Stir in the curry paste and cook for 1 minute.

4 Add the coconut milk, stock and aubergine, then return the chicken to the pan. Simmer for 10 minutes. Add the noodles and cook for a further 5 minutes, or until the chicken is cooked and the noodles are tender. Stir in the coriander and lemon juice and adjust the seasoning. Serve garnished with coriander.

Cook's Tip
If you like, stir in a little Thai fish sauce just before serving.

Chinese Chicken with Cashew Nuts

Marinating the chicken gives it a really marvellous flavour and makes it melt-in-the-mouth tender.

Serves 4

4 skinless, boneless chicken breast portions, 175g/6oz each, sliced into strips
3 garlic cloves, crushed
60ml/4 tbsp soy sauce
30ml/2 tbsp cornflour (cornstarch)
225g/8oz dried egg noodles
45ml/3 tbsp groundnut (peanut) or sunflower oil
15ml/1 tbsp sesame oil
115g/4oz/1 cup roasted cashew nuts
6 spring onions (scallions), cut into 5cm/2in pieces and halved lengthways
salt
spring onion (scallion) curls and a little chopped fresh red chilli, to garnish

1 Put the chicken strips in a bowl and add the garlic, soy sauce and cornflour. Mix until the chicken is well coated. Cover and chill for about 30 minutes.

2 Meanwhile, bring a pan of lightly salted water to the boil. Add the egg noodles. Turn off the heat and leave to stand for 5 minutes. Drain well and reserve.

3 Preheat a wok. Add the groundnut or sunflower and sesame oils. When they are hot, add the chilled chicken, with the marinade. Stir-fry over a high heat for 3–4 minutes, or until golden brown. Add the cashew nuts and spring onions to the wok, and stir-fry for 2–3 minutes.

4 Add the drained noodles and toss over the heat for about 2 minutes more, or until the noodles are hot. Serve, garnished with the spring onion curls and chopped chilli.

Cook's Tip
To make spring onion (scallion) curls, trim the green part and cut off the bulb. Make a series of lengthways cuts in the stem to within 5mm/¼in of one end. Place in iced water until curled.

VEGETARIAN PASTA

You don't have to be a committed vegetarian to enjoy these flavoursome dishes, as pasta has a natural affinity with cheese, cream, vegetables, mushrooms, herbs and the many other ingredients that take a starring role in this chapter. Recipes range from simple classics, such as Fettuccine all'Alfredo, to fabulous new ideas, such as Cheat's Lasagne with Mixed Mushrooms. There are robust and filling bakes, sophisticated dinner-party dishes, quick and easy midweek suppers and light, fresh-tasting combinations perfect for an *al fresco* lunch. From rich and creamy Macaroni with Four Cheeses to colourful and spicy Spaghettini with Garlic & Chilli Oil and from unpretentious and basic Spaghetti Olio e Aglio to luxurious and aromatic Tagliarini with White Truffle, there is something to suit all tastes, occasions and budgets. Many of these delicious dishes can be made in minutes – ideal for today's rushed and often frantic lifestyle – while those who have time to be creative in the kitchen will enjoy making their own fresh ravioli with a choice of tasty vegetable fillings. As an additional bonus, this chapter is a reminder of the pleasures of seasonal cooking – rediscover the magical flavour of summer's sun-ripened tomatoes, the sweetness of freshly podded young peas, the crispness of tender springtime vegetables and the tantalizing pepperiness of rocket (arugula).

Spaghetti Olio e Aglio

Proof positive that you don't need numerous ingredients to make a tasty dish.

Serves 4

120ml/4fl oz/ ½ cup olive oil
2 garlic cloves, crushed
450g/1lb dried spaghetti
30ml/2 tbsp fresh parsley, roughly chopped
salt and freshly ground black pepper

1 Heat the olive oil in a medium pan and add the garlic and a pinch of salt. Cook over a low heat, stirring constantly, until golden. Do not allow the garlic to become too brown or it will taste bitter.

2 Meanwhile, bring a large pan of lightly salted water to the boil and cook the spaghetti until *al dente*.

3 Drain the spaghetti well, return it to the clean pan and add the warm – not sizzling – garlic and oil with plenty of black pepper and the parsley. Toss to coat. Serve immediately, in warmed bowls.

Cook's Tips

• Don't be tempted to serve this with grated Parmesan. Its pure taste would be compromised.
• The most commonly exported Italian olive oil comes from Tuscany. It is full-bodied with a slight peppery aftertaste. Ligurian oil has a sweeter and more delicate flavour and is ideal for this dish. Olive oil from the south of Italy has a faint almond-like flavour. It is worth buying the best-quality extra virgin olive oil for this classic Roman dish.

Spaghettini with Garlic & Chilli Oil

It is essential to use a good-quality extra virgin olive oil and a brightly coloured red chilli for this simply delicious pasta sauce.

Serves 4

350g/12oz dried spaghettini
75ml/5 tbsp extra virgin olive oil
3 garlic cloves, finely chopped
1 fresh red chilli, seeded and chopped
75g/3oz/ ¾ cup drained sun-dried tomatoes in oil, chopped
30ml/2 tbsp chopped fresh parsley
salt and freshly ground black pepper
freshly grated Parmesan cheese, to serve

1 Bring a large pan of lightly salted water to the boil. Add the pasta and cook until *al dente*.

2 Towards the end of the cooking time, heat the oil in a large pan. Add the garlic and chilli, and cook gently for 2–3 minutes. Stir in the sun-dried tomatoes and remove from the heat.

3 Drain the pasta and add it to the hot sauce. Return to the heat and cook for 2–3 minutes, tossing the pasta to coat the strands. Season with salt and pepper, and stir in the parsley. Serve in warmed bowls, topped with the grated Parmesan.

Variation

For a smoother sauce and a slight change of flavour, tip the contents of a 200g/7oz jar of sun-dried tomatoes into a food processor, and add two smoked garlic cloves and 5–10ml 1–2 tsp dried red chilli flakes. Process to a smooth purée and season with salt and pepper. Toss with the freshly cooked pasta and serve garnished with eight sliced pitted black olives.

Linguine with Pesto

Pesto is traditionally made with a mortar and pestle, but it is much easier to use a food processor.

Serves 5–6

65g/2½oz/2½ cups fresh basil leaves, plus extra to garnish
3–4 garlic cloves, peeled
45ml/3 tbsp pine nuts
2.5ml/ ½ tsp salt
75ml/5 tbsp olive oil
50g/2oz/ ⅔ cup freshly grated Parmesan cheese
60ml/4 tbsp freshly grated Pecorino cheese
500g/1¼lb fresh or dried linguine
freshly ground black pepper

1 Place the basil, garlic, pine nuts, salt and olive oil in a blender or food processor and process until smooth. Scrape into a bowl and stir in the cheeses. Season with pepper.

2 Bring a large pan of lightly salted water to the boil and cook the pasta until it is *al dente*. Just before draining it, remove about 60ml/4 tbsp of the cooking water and stir it into the basil mixture.

3 Drain the pasta and return it to the clean pan. Add the basil pesto and toss to coat. Serve immediately, garnished with the basil sprigs.

Variations

• *Traditional Ligurian pesto does not contain pine nuts and is made using all Pecorino, rather than a mixture of cheeses. In addition, 75–115g/3–4oz green beans and 75g/3oz/ ¼ cup diced potato are cooked with the pasta.*
• *For a more aromatic pesto, dry-fry the pine nuts in a heavy frying pan, stirring frequently, for 1–2 minutes before mixing them with the other ingredients.*
• *For a milder, creamier pesto, stir in 30ml/2 tbsp Greek (US strained plain) yogurt instead of the pasta water.*
• *For walnut pesto, substitute 25g/1oz/ ¼ cup shelled walnuts for the pine nuts.*

Spaghetti with Rocket Pesto

This is the pesto for real rocket lovers. It is sharp and peppery, and delicious for a summer pasta meal with a glass of chilled white wine.

Serves 4

4 garlic cloves
90ml/6 tbsp pine nuts
150g/5oz rocket (arugula), stalks removed
50g/2oz/ ⅔ cup freshly grated Parmesan cheese
50g/2oz/ ⅔ cup freshly grated Pecorino cheese
90ml/6 tbsp extra virgin olive oil
400g/14oz fresh or dried spaghetti
salt and freshly ground black pepper
freshly grated Parmesan and Pecorino cheese, to serve

1 Put the garlic and pine nuts in a blender or food processor and process until finely chopped.

2 Add the rocket, Parmesan and Pecorino, and process for 5 seconds. With the motor running, gradually add the olive oil, pouring it through the hole in the lid or the feeder tube. Stop and scrape down the side of the bowl. Season and process for 5–10 seconds more until smooth.

3 Meanwhile, bring a large pan of lightly salted water to the boil and cook the spaghetti until *al dente*.

4 Just before the pasta is ready, scrape the pesto into a large bowl, add 60ml/4 tbsp of the cooking water from the pasta and stir well to mix.

5 Drain the pasta, tip it into the bowl of pesto and toss well. Serve immediately, with the grated cheeses handed separately.

Variation

To temper the flavour of the rocket and make the pesto milder, stir 115g/4oz/ ½ cup ricotta or mascarpone cheese into the pesto before adding the cooking water and tossing the sauce with the pasta.

Spaghetti with Fresh Tomato Sauce

This is traditionally made in high summer, when tomatoes are very ripe and sweet. It is deliberately kept simple, so that nothing detracts from the pure tomato flavour.

Serves 4

60ml/4 tbsp olive oil
1 onion, finely chopped
675g/1½ lb ripe Italian plum tomatoes, peeled and chopped
350g/12oz fresh or dried spaghetti
a small handful of fresh basil leaves, shredded
salt and freshly ground black pepper
coarsely shaved Parmesan cheese, to serve

1 Heat the oil in a large pan, add the onion and cook over a low heat, stirring frequently, for about 5 minutes, until softened and lightly coloured. Add the tomatoes, with salt and pepper to taste. Cover and simmer, stirring occasionally, for 30–40 minutes, until thick.

2 Meanwhile, bring a pan of lightly salted water to the boil and cook the pasta until it is *al dente*.

3 Drain the pasta, tip it into a warmed bowl, pour the sauce over, add the basil and toss well. Serve in warmed bowls with shaved Parmesan handed separately.

Cook's Tips

• The Italian plum tomatoes called San Marzano are the best variety to use. When fully ripe, they have thin skins that can be peeled off easily.

• To peel tomatoes, cut a cross in the blossom of each one, then plunge them into boiling water for about 30 seconds. Lift them out with a slotted spoon. The skin will have begun to peel back from the crosses and will be easy to remove.

• An alternative method is to spear each tomato in turn with a long-handled fork and hold it in a flame, turning it until the skin chars slightly and splits.

Bucatini with Raw Tomato Sauce

This is a wonderfully simple uncooked tomato sauce that goes well with both long pasta strands and small, chunky shapes.

Serves 4

500g/1¼ lb ripe Italian plum tomatoes
1 large handful fresh basil leaves
75ml/5 tbsp extra virgin olive oil
1 garlic clove, crushed
350g/2oz fresh or dried bucatini
115g/4oz ricotta salata cheese, diced
salt and freshly ground black pepper
coarsely shaved Pecorino cheese, to serve

1 Roughly chop the plum tomatoes, removing the cores and as many of the seeds as you can. Tear the basil leaves into shreds with your fingers.

2 Put the tomatoes, basil, olive oil and garlic in a bowl and season with salt and pepper to taste. Stir well to mix, cover and then leave at room temperature for 1–2 hours to let the flavours mingle.

3 Bring a large pan of lightly salted water to the boil and cook the pasta until it is *al dente*.

4 Drain the pasta and return it to the clean pan. Add the raw tomato sauce and the ricotta salata and toss to coat. Serve immediately, with shavings of Pecorino cheese.

Cook's Tips

• Ricotta salata is a salted and dried version of ricotta cheese made from the whey of Pecorino. It is firmer than the traditional soft white ricotta, with a compact, flaky texture. It can be easily diced, crumbled and even grated. It is available from some delicatessens. If you can't locate it, you can use feta cheese instead.

• If fresh plum tomatoes are not available, use vine-ripened round tomatoes instead.

Pasta with Mushrooms & Sun-dried Tomatoes

Served with warm ciabatta, this makes an excellent vegetarian supper dish.

Serves 4

15g/½oz dried porcini mushrooms
175ml/6fl oz/ ¾ cup hot water
45ml/3 tbsp olive oil
2 garlic cloves, finely chopped
a handful of fresh flat leaf parsley, roughly chopped
2 large pieces sun-dried tomato in olive oil, drained and sliced into thin strips
120ml/4fl oz/ ½ cup dry white wine
225g/8oz/3 cups chestnut mushrooms, thinly sliced
475ml/16fl oz/2 cups vegetable stock
450g/1lb/4 cups dried short pasta shapes
salt and freshly ground black pepper
rocket (arugula) and fresh flat leaf parsley, to garnish

1 Put the porcini mushrooms in a bowl, pour the hot water over and soak for 15 minutes. Tip into a sieve set over a bowl and squeeze the porcini to release as much liquid as possible. Reserve the strained soaking liquid. Chop the porcini finely.

2 Heat the oil in a frying pan and cook the garlic, parsley, sun-dried tomato strips and porcini over a low heat, stirring frequently, for about 5 minutes. Stir in the wine, simmer for a few minutes until reduced, then add the chestnut mushrooms. Pour in the stock and simmer for 15–20 minutes more until the liquid has reduced and the sauce is quite thick and rich.

3 Meanwhile, bring a large pan of lightly salted water to the boil and cook the pasta shapes until they are *al dente*.

4 Taste the mushroom sauce for seasoning. Drain the pasta, reserving a little of the cooking liquid, and tip it into a warmed large bowl. Add the mushroom sauce and toss well, thinning the sauce if necessary with some of the pasta cooking water. Serve immediately, sprinkled with chopped rocket and parsley.

Fusilli with Wild Mushrooms & Herbs

A very rich dish with an earthy flavour and lots of garlic, this makes an ideal main course, especially if it is followed by a crisp green salad of mixed leaves.

Serves 4

½ x 275g/10oz jar wild mushrooms in olive oil
25g/1oz/2 tbsp butter
225g/8oz/3 cups fresh wild mushrooms, sliced if large
5ml/1 tsp finely chopped fresh thyme
5ml/1 tsp finely chopped fresh marjoram or oregano, plus extra herbs to serve
4 garlic cloves, crushed
350g/12oz/3 cups fresh or dried fusilli
200ml/7fl oz/scant 1 cup double (heavy) cream
salt and freshly ground black pepper

1 Drain about 15ml/1 tbsp of the oil from the bottled mushrooms into a medium pan. Slice or chop the fresh mushrooms into bitesize pieces, if they are large.

2 Add the butter to the oil in the pan and heat until sizzling. Add the bottled and fresh mushrooms, thyme, marjoram or oregano and garlic and season with salt and pepper to taste. Simmer, stirring frequently, for 10 minutes, or until the fresh mushrooms are soft and tender.

3 Meanwhile, bring a large pan of lightly salted water to the boil and cook the fusilli until they are *al dente*.

4 As soon as the mushrooms are cooked, increase the heat to high and toss the mixture with a wooden spoon to drive off any excess liquid. Pour in the double cream and bring to the boil, stirring constantly, then taste and add more salt and pepper if necessary.

5 Drain the pasta and tip it into a warmed bowl. Pour the sauce over and toss well. Serve immediately, sprinkled with extra fresh marjoram or oregano leaves.

Conchiglie with Roasted Vegetables

Nothing could be simpler than tossing pasta with roasted vegetables. The flavour is superb.

Serves 4–6

1 red (bell) pepper, seeded and cut into 1cm/ ½in squares
1 yellow or orange (bell) pepper, seeded and cut into 1cm/ ½in squares
1 small aubergine (eggplant), coarsely diced
2 courgettes (zucchini), coarsely diced
75ml/5 tbsp extra virgin olive oil
15ml/1 tbsp chopped fresh flat leaf parsley
5ml/1 tsp dried oregano or marjoram
250g/9oz baby Italian plum tomatoes, halved lengthways
2 garlic cloves, coarsely chopped
350–400g/12–14oz/3–3½ cups dried conchiglie
salt and freshly ground black pepper
4–6 fresh marjoram or oregano flowers, to garnish

1 Preheat the oven to 190°C/375°F/Gas 5. Put the peppers, aubergine and courgettes in a bowl, add 45ml/3 tbsp of the olive oil and stir to coat the vegetables. Tip them into a large roasting pan and spread them out. Sprinkle the fresh and dried herbs over the vegetables. Add salt and pepper to taste and stir well. Roast for 30 minutes, stirring two to three times.

2 Stir the tomatoes and chopped garlic into the vegetable mixture, then roast for 20 minutes more, stirring once or twice.

3 Meanwhile, bring a large pan of lightly salted water to the boil and cook the pasta until *al dente*.

4 Drain the pasta and tip it into a warmed bowl. Add the vegetables with any liquid in the roasting pan. Add the remaining oil and toss well. Serve, sprinkled with herb flowers.

Variation
This mixture makes a marvellous filling for pitta pockets, especially if you use small pasta shapes.

Vermicelli Frittata

A frittata is a flat, baked omelette. It is absolutely delicious cold. Cut into wedges, it makes excellent picnic fare.

Serves 4–6

50g/2oz dried vermicelli
6 eggs
60ml/4 tbsp double (heavy) cream
a handful of fresh basil leaves, shredded
a handful of fresh flat leaf parsley, chopped
75g/3oz/1 cup freshly grated Parmesan cheese
25g/1oz/2 tbsp butter
15ml/1 tbsp olive oil
1 onion, thinly sliced
3 large pieces of drained bottled roasted red (bell) pepper, cut into strips
1 garlic clove, crushed
salt and freshly ground black pepper
rocket (arugula) leaves, to serve

1 Preheat the oven to 190°C/375°F/Gas 5. Bring a small pan of lightly salted water to the boil and cook the pasta until *al dente*.

2 Meanwhile, beat the eggs with the cream and herbs in a bowl. Whisk in about two-thirds of the grated Parmesan and add salt and pepper to taste.

3 Drain the pasta well and allow to cool; snip it into short lengths. Add it to the egg mixture and whisk again. Set aside.

4 Melt the butter in the oil in a large non-stick frying pan that can be safely used in the oven. Fry the onion over a low heat, for 5 minutes, until softened. Add the peppers and garlic. Pour the egg and pasta mixture into the pan and stir to make sure that the pasta is evenly distributed. Cook over a low to medium heat, without stirring, for 3–5 minutes, or until the frittata is just set underneath.

5 Sprinkle over the remaining Parmesan and transfer the pan to the oven. Bake for 5 minutes, or until set. Before serving, leave to stand for at least 5 minutes. Cut into wedges and serve warm or cold with rocket.

Fettuccine all'Alfredo

A classic dish from Rome, Fettuccine all'Alfredo is simply pasta tossed with cream, butter and freshly grated Parmesan cheese. It is incredibly quick and simple, perfect for a midweek supper

Serves 4
450g/1lb dried fettuccine
25g/1oz/2 tbsp butter
200ml/7fl oz/scant 1 cup double (heavy) cream
50g/2oz/ ⅔ cup freshly grated Parmesan cheese, plus extra to serve
freshly grated nutmeg
salt and freshly ground black pepper
fresh dill sprigs or chopped fresh flat leaf parsley to garnish

1 Bring a large pan of lightly salted water to the boil and cook the pasta. Allow slightly less time than usual; it should be almost *al dente*, but still slightly firm.

2 Meanwhile, melt the butter with 150ml/ ¼ pint/ ⅔ cup of the cream in a heavy pan. Bring to the boil, then lower the heat and simmer for 1 minute, until slightly thickened. Leave over the lowest possible heat.

3 Drain the pasta very well and add it to the cream sauce. Keeping the heat low, toss the pasta in the sauce.

4 Add the remaining cream with the Parmesan and season with salt and pepper to taste. Grate in a little nutmeg. Toss until well coated and heated through. Serve immediately, garnished with dill or parsley and with extra freshly grated Parmesan.

Cook's Tip
While fettuccine is traditional, this sauce also goes well with tagliatelle. Pasta shapes, such as penne, rigatoni or farfalle, are also suitable.

Creamy Pasta with Parmesan Curls

Several perfectly formed curls of Parmesan give a plate of creamy pasta a lift.

Serves 4–6
250g/9oz/2¼ cups dried campanelle
250g/9oz/generous 1 cup mascarpone cheese
200ml/7fl oz/scant 1 cup crème fraîche
75g/3oz/1 cup freshly grated Parmesan cheese
115g/4oz/2 cups sun-dried tomatoes in oil, drained and thinly sliced
salt and freshly ground black pepper

To garnish
1 piece of Parmesan cheese, about 175g/6oz

1 Unless you are an old hand at making Parmesan curls, do this first, before cooking the pasta. Holding a swivel-blade vegetable peeler at a 45° angle, draw it steadily across the block of Parmesan cheese to form a curl. Make several curls, depending on the number of guests being served.

2 Bring a large pan of lightly salted water to the boil and cook the pasta until it is *al dente*.

3 Meanwhile, put the mascarpone and crème fraîche in a second pan and heat gently until the mascarpone has melted. Add the Parmesan and sun-dried tomatoes, and cook over a low heat for 5 minutes. Season with salt and pepper.

4 Drain the pasta, return it to the clean pan and pour the sauce over. Toss to mix thoroughly. Serve immediately on warmed individual plates, adding a few Parmesan curls to garnish each portion.

Cook's Tip
Mascarpone is a very rich cheese, containing 90 per cent fat. A lighter version, called fiorello light, is now being made. While this is suitable for the health-conscious on a low-fat diet, it is not so delicious as the genuine article.

Paglia e Fieno

The title of this dish translates as "straw and hay" which refers to the yellow and green colours of the pasta when mixed together. Using fresh peas makes all the difference to this dish.

Serves 4

450g/1lb dried paglia e fieno (egg- and spinach-flavoured tagliatelle)
50g/2oz/ ¼ cup butter
900g/2lb fresh peas in the pod, shelled
200ml/7fl oz/scant 1 cup double (heavy) cream
50g/2oz/ ⅔ cup freshly grated Parmesan cheese, plus extra to serve
freshly grated nutmeg
salt and freshly ground black pepper

1 Bring a large pan of lightly salted water to the boil and cook the pasta until it is *al dente*.

2 Meanwhile, melt the butter in a heavy pan and add the peas. Sauté for 2–3 minutes, stirring occasionally, then stir in 150ml/ ¼ pint/ ⅔ cup of the cream. Bring to the boil, then lower the heat and simmer until slightly thickened.

3 Drain the pasta and add it to the pan containing the cream and pea sauce. Toss briefly to mix.

4 Pour in the remaining cream. Add the cheese and season to taste with salt, pepper and a little grated nutmeg. Toss over a gentle heat until well coated and heated through. Serve immediately, with extra Parmesan cheese.

Variation
Sautéed mushrooms make a good addition.

Tagliatelle with Baby Vegetables

Make this in the spring, when there are plenty of baby vegetables in markets or on farm stalls.

Serves 4

30ml/2 tbsp olive oil
115g/4oz baby carrots, halved lengthways
115g/4oz baby aubergines (eggplants), halved lengthways
115g/4oz baby courgettes (zucchini), halved lengthways
2 garlic cloves, chopped
15ml/1 tbsp chopped fresh rosemary, plus fresh rosemary sprigs to garnish
300ml/ ½ pint/1 ¼ cups single (light) cream
350g/12oz fresh tagliatelle
salt and freshly ground black pepper

1 Heat the oil in a large, heavy frying pan. Add the carrots, aubergines, courgettes, garlic and chopped rosemary and cook over a gentle heat, covered, for 20–30 minutes, until browned, stirring occasionally.

2 Remove the pan from the heat and stir in the cream, scraping any sediment from the bottom of the pan. Season to taste with salt and pepper. Return the pan to a low heat and cook for about 4 minutes more until heated through.

3 Meanwhile, bring a large pan of lightly salted water to the boil and cook the pasta until *al dente*.

4 Drain the pasta thoroughly and return it to the clean pan. Add the vegetable mixture and toss thoroughly to coat. Serve immediately, garnished with fresh rosemary.

Variation
Mix and match the vegetables, according to what is available. If you are lucky enough to take part in an organic box scheme, ask your supplier for the youngest, freshest vegetables around. Patty pan squash, mangetouts (snow peas) or baby parsnips could be used. Just make sure that the total quantity is about 350g/12oz.

Baked Macaroni Cheese

A few refinements turn a family favourite into a dish that would be ideal for a supper with friends.

Serves 4

275g/10oz/2½ cups dried short-cut macaroni
2 leeks, chopped
50g/2oz/ ¼ cup butter
50g/2oz/ ½ cup plain (all-purpose) flour
900ml/1½ pints/3¼ cups milk
225g/8oz/2 cups grated mature (sharp) Cheddar cheese
30ml/2 tbsp fromage frais or cream cheese
5ml/1 tsp wholegrain mustard
50g/2oz/1 cup fresh white breadcrumbs
25g/1oz/ ¼ cup grated double Gloucester cheese
salt and freshly ground black pepper
15ml/1 tbsp chopped fresh parsley, to garnish

1 Preheat the oven to 180°C/350°F/Gas 4. Bring a large pan of lightly salted water to the boil and cook the macaroni with the leeks until the macaroni is *al dente*. Drain, rinse under cold water and set aside.

2 Heat the butter in a pan, add the flour and cook, stirring constantly, for 1–2 minutes. Gradually add the milk, continuing to stir until the sauce boils and thickens. Add the Cheddar cheese, fromage frais or cream cheese and mustard, mix well and season with salt and pepper to taste.

3 Stir the drained macaroni and leeks into the cheese sauce and pile into a greased ovenproof dish. Level the top with the back of a spoon, and sprinkle over the breadcrumbs and double Gloucester cheese. Bake for 35–40 minutes until the topping is golden and bubbling. Serve immediately, garnished with the fresh parsley.

Variations
Use broccoli or cauliflower instead of leeks, or leave out the vegetables altogether and arrange tomato slices around the rim of the bake, with the crumb mixture confined to the centre.

Macaroni with Four Cheeses

Rich and creamy, this is a deluxe macaroni cheese that goes well with either a tomato and basil salad or dressed green leaves.

Serves 4

250g/9oz/2¼ cups short-cut macaroni
50g/2oz/ ¼ cup butter
50g/2oz/ ½ cup plain (all-purpose) flour
600ml/1 pint/2½ cups milk
120ml/4fl oz/ ½ cup double (heavy) cream
90ml/6 tbsp dry white wine
50g/2oz/ ½ cup grated Gruyère or Emmenthal cheese
50g/2oz Fontina cheese, diced small
50g/2oz Gorgonzola cheese, crumbled
75g/3oz/1 cup freshly grated Parmesan cheese
salt and freshly ground black pepper
green salad, to serve

1 Preheat the oven to 180°C/350°F/Gas 4. Bring a large pan of lightly salted water to the boil and cook the macaroni until it is *al dente*.

2 Meanwhile, melt the butter in a heavy pan over a low heat. Add the flour and cook, stirring constantly, for 1–2 minutes. Add the milk a little at a time, whisking vigorously after each addition. Stir in the cream, followed by the dry white wine. Bring to the boil, stirring constantly. Cook, stirring constantly, until the sauce thickens, then remove the pan from the heat.

3 Add the Gruyère or Emmenthal, the Fontina, Gorgonzola and about one-third of the grated Parmesan to the sauce. Stir well to mix in the cheeses, then taste for seasoning and add salt and pepper if necessary.

4 Drain the pasta well and tip it into an ovenproof dish. Pour the sauce over the pasta and mix well, then sprinkle the remaining Parmesan over the top.

5 Transfer the dish to the oven and bake for 25–30 minutes, or until golden brown. Serve hot with a green salad.

Tagliarini with White Truffle

There is nothing quite like the fragrance and flavour of the Italian white truffle. This simple style of serving it is one of the best ways to enjoy it.

Serves 4

350g/12oz fresh tagliarini
75g/3oz/6 tbsp unsalted (sweet) butter, diced
60ml/4 tbsp freshly grated Parmesan cheese
freshly grated nutmeg
1 small white truffle, about 25–40g/1–1½oz
salt and freshly ground black pepper

1 Bring a large pan of lightly salted water to the boil and cook the pasta until it is *al dente*.

2 Drain the pasta thoroughly and tip it into a warmed large bowl. Add the diced butter and grated Parmesan. Grate in a little nutmeg, and add salt and pepper to taste. Toss well until the pasta is coated in melted butter and cheese.

3 Divide the pasta equally among four warmed bowls and carefully shave paper-thin slivers of the white truffle on top. Serve immediately.

Cook's Tip

White Italian truffles can be bought during the months of September and October from specialist food shops and delicatessens. They are very expensive, however, and there are some alternative ways of getting the flavour of truffles without the expense. Some Italian delicatessens sell "truffle cheese", which is a mountain of cheese with shavings of truffle in it, and this can be used instead of the Parmesan and fresh truffle in this recipe. Another alternative is to toss hot pasta in truffle oil and serve it with freshly grated Parmesan. Canned and bottled truffles and – a less expensive alternative – truffle pieces are also available. Use the oil to flavour egg or rice dishes.

Cheat's Lasagne with Mixed Mushrooms

This vegetarian version of lasagne requires neither baking nor the preparation of various sauces and fillings.

Serves 4

40g/1½oz/⅔ cup dried porcini mushrooms
60ml/4 tbsp olive oil
1 large garlic clove, chopped
375g/13oz/5 cups mixed mushrooms, including brown cap, field (portabello), shiitake and wild varieties, roughly sliced
175ml/6fl oz/¾ cup dry white wine
90ml/6 tbsp canned chopped tomatoes
2.5ml/½ tsp granulated sugar
8 fresh lasagne sheets
40g/1½oz/½ cup freshly grated Parmesan cheese
salt and freshly ground black pepper
fresh basil leaves, to garnish

1 Place the porcini in a bowl and cover with boiling water. Leave to soak for 15 minutes, then drain and rinse.

2 Heat the oil in a large, heavy frying pan and sauté the porcini over a high heat for 5 minutes until the edges are just crisp. Reduce the heat, add the garlic and fresh mushrooms. Sauté for 5 minutes more, until tender, stirring occasionally.

3 Add the wine and cook for 5–7 minutes until reduced. Stir in the tomatoes, sugar and seasoning and cook over a medium heat for about 5 minutes, until thickened.

4 Meanwhile, bring a large pan of lightly salted water to the boil and cook the lasagne until it is *al dente*. Drain.

5 To serve, spoon a little of the mushroom sauce on to each of four warm serving plates. Place a sheet of lasagne on top and spoon one-quarter of the remaining mushroom sauce over each serving. Sprinkle with some Parmesan and top with another pasta sheet. Sprinkle with black pepper and the remaining Parmesan and garnish with the basil leaves.

Spinach & Dolcelatte Ravioli

The filling for these ravioli is superb and does justice to the home-made pasta.

Serves 4–6

200g/7oz/1¾ cups strong unbleached white bread flour
2 eggs, beaten
pinch of salt
melted butter, chopped fresh parsley and Parmesan shavings, to serve

For the filling

225g/8oz fresh spinach leaves
25g/1oz/2 tbsp butter
1 small onion, finely chopped
25g/1oz/⅓ cup freshly grated Parmesan cheese
40g/1½oz dolcelatte cheese, crumbled
salt and freshly ground black pepper

1 Place the flour, beaten eggs and salt in a food processor. Pulse to combine, then transfer the dough to a lightly floured surface and knead for 5 minutes, until smooth.

2 Divide the pasta into four pieces and flatten slightly. Using a pasta machine on its thinnest setting, roll out each piece. Leave the sheets on clean dishtowels to dry slightly.

3 Meanwhile, make the filling. Wash the spinach, then place it in a heavy pan with just the water that clings to the leaves. Cover and cook until wilted, then drain well, pressing out the excess liquid. Chop finely and put in a bowl. Melt the butter in a small pan and fry the onion until soft. Add to the spinach with the cheeses. Season well and leave to cool.

4 Place small scoops of the filling on one of the pasta sheets in neat rows about 4cm/1½in apart. Brush the pasta with water, place another sheet on top and press down around each scoop of filling. Cut out the ravioli. Make more ravioli in the same way, then leave them all to rest for 15 minutes.

5 Bring a large pan of lightly salted water to the boil and cook the ravioli for 4–5 minutes. Drain well, then toss with melted butter and parsley. Divide among four warmed serving plates, sprinkle with shavings of Parmesan and serve.

Ravioli with Swiss Chard

Only the leaves of the chard are used for this tasty dish.

Serves 4–6

200g/7oz/1¾ cups strong unbleached white bread flour
2 eggs, beaten
pinch of salt

For the filling

350g/12oz Swiss chard
60ml/4 tbsp water
115g/4oz/⅔ cup ricotta cheese
45ml/3 tbsp freshly grated Parmesan cheese
pinch of freshly grated nutmeg
milk (optional)
salt and freshly ground black pepper

For the sauce

75g/3oz/6 tbsp butter
leaves from 5–6 fresh sage sprigs

1 Place the flour, eggs and salt in a food processor. Pulse to combine, then transfer the dough to a lightly floured surface and knead for 5 minutes, until smooth.

2 Divide the pasta into four pieces and flatten slightly. Using a pasta machine on its thinnest setting, roll out each piece. Leave the sheets on clean dishtowels to dry slightly.

3 Meanwhile, make the filling. Trim the chard, separating the leaves from the stems. Chop the leaves finely and place them in a heavy pan with the water. Cover and cook until wilted, then drain well, pressing out the excess liquid. Mash the ricotta with the Parmesan, nutmeg and seasoning. Add the chard and mix well. If the mixture seems slightly thick, add a little milk.

4 Place small scoops of the filling on one of the pasta sheets in neat rows about 4cm/1½in apart. Brush the pasta with water, place another sheet on top and press down around each scoop of filling. Cut out the ravioli. Make more ravioli in the same way, then leave them all to rest for 15 minutes.

5 Bring a large pan of lightly salted water to the boil and cook the ravioli for 4–5 minutes. Meanwhile, make the sauce by melting the butter with the sage leaves. Drain the ravioli well and arrange in warmed dishes. Spoon on the sauce and serve.

Ravioli with Four Cheese Sauce

This has a smooth, rich sauce that coats the pasta very evenly.

Serves 4

350g/12oz/3 cups fresh ravioli
50g/2oz/ ¼ cup butter
50g/2oz/ ½ cup plain (all-purpose) flour
450ml/ ¾ pint/scant 2 cups milk
50g/2oz fresh Parmesan cheese
50g/2oz Edam cheese
50g/2oz Gruyère cheese
50g/2oz Fontina cheese
salt and freshly ground black pepper
chopped fresh flat leaf parsley, to garnish

1 Bring a large pan of lightly salted water to the boil and cook the pasta until it is *al dente*.

2 Meanwhile, melt the butter in a heavy pan over a low heat. Stir in the flour and cook for 1–2 minutes, stirring constantly. Gradually add the milk, stirring constantly until the sauce boils and thickens.

3 Grate all the cheeses and stir them into the sauce until they are just beginning to melt. Remove the pan from the heat and season the sauce with salt and pepper to taste.

4 Drain the ravioli thoroughly and tip it into a large serving bowl. Pour over the sauce and toss to coat. Serve immediately, garnished with the chopped fresh parsley.

Cook's Tips

• Buy the ravioli from your favourite fresh pasta retailer, or make your own, following the instructions in the Techniques section. Alternatively, serve the sauce over tortellini.

• The sauce would go well with almost all vegetarian fillings, from mushrooms to sun-dried tomatoes.

• As the cheeses are such a feature of the recipe, it is worth buying them from a delicatessen, if possible, rather than plastic-wrapped from a supermarket. Buy the Parmesan in a single piece rather than ready grated.

Spicy Cheese Lasagne

Adding a chilli and hot pepper flakes peps up a dish that is sometimes in danger of being a little bland.

Serves 8

50g/2oz/ ¼ cup butter, plus extra for greasing
1 large onion, finely chopped
3 garlic cloves, crushed
1 small fresh green chilli
50g/2oz/ ½ cup plain (all-purpose) flour
1 litre/1¾ pints/4 cups milk
2 x 400g/14oz cans chopped tomatoes
1 large courgette (zucchini), sliced
2.5ml/ ½ tsp hot red pepper flakes
12–16 fresh lasagne sheets, precooked if necessary, or no-precook dried lasagne
350g/12oz/3 cups grated mature (sharp) Cheddar cheese
salt and freshly ground black pepper
fresh parsley, to garnish

1 Preheat the oven to 190°C/375°F/Gas 5. Grease a large ovenproof dish.

2 Melt the butter in a large pan. Add the onion, garlic and chilli, and cook over a low heat, stirring occasionally, for about 5 minutes, until softened.

3 Stir in the flour and cook for 1–2 minutes, stirring constantly. Gradually add the milk, stirring constantly until the sauce boils and thickens.

4 Stir the tomatoes, courgette and hot pepper flakes into the sauce. Season with salt and pepper.

5 Spoon a little of the sauce into the prepared ovenproof dish and spread it evenly over the base. Cover with a layer of lasagne sheets.

6 Add one-third of the remaining sauce and one-third of the grated cheese. Repeat the layers until all the ingredients have been used. Bake for about 45 minutes, until the top is golden and bubbling. Leave to stand for 10 minutes before serving garnished with parsley.

Soft Fried Noodles

This is a very basic dish that may be served as an accompaniment or on those occasions when you are feeling a little peckish and fancy something simple.

Serves 4–6

350g/12oz dried egg noodles
30ml/2 tbsp vegetable oil
30ml/2 tbsp finely chopped spring onions (scallions)
soy sauce, to taste
salt and freshly ground black pepper

1 Bring a large pan of lightly salted water to the boil and cook the noodles until just tender. Drain, rinse under cold running water and drain again thoroughly.

2 Preheat a wok. Pour in the vegetable oil and swirl it around. Add the spring onions and stir-fry for 30 seconds over a medium heat. Add the drained noodles, stirring gently to separate the strands.

3 Reduce the heat to low and stir-fry the noodles, turning and tossing constantly, until they are heated through and lightly browned and crisp on the outside, but still soft and tender inside. Long chopsticks are ideal for turning the noodles, or use two wooden spatulas.

4 Tip the noodles into a warmed serving dish and season with soy sauce, salt and pepper. Serve immediately.

Variations

- *If you want to add protein, break an egg into the noodles and stir until lightly scrambled.*
- *The noodles are also good tossed with a teaspoon of chilli black bean sauce.*
- *For a more substantial dish, stir-fry 115g/4oz/scant 1 cup very thinly sliced cauliflower florets before cooking the spring onions (scallions). Add 15ml/1 tbsp yellow bean sauce and 10ml/2 tsp brown sugar and heat through just before serving.*

Loopy Noodle Nests

Serve these with stir-fries or as a crunchy snack.

Makes 4–6 nests

175g/6oz flat ribbon noodles
oil, for deep-frying

1 Bring a large pan of lightly salted water to the boil and cook the noodles until *al dente*. Drain, rinse under cold water and drain again. Blot dry on kitchen paper.
2 Heat the oil for deep-frying to 190°C/375°F. Using a spoon and fork, swirl the noodles into nests.
3 Carefully lower each nest in turn into the oil. Deep-fry for about 3–4 minutes, or until golden. Drain on kitchen paper.

Noodles with Ginger & Coriander

Here is a simple noodle dish that goes well with most Asian dishes. It can also be served as a snack for two to three people.

Serves 2–6

a handful of fresh coriander (cilantro) sprigs
225g/8oz dried egg noodles
45ml/3 tbsp groundnut (peanut) oil
5cm/2in piece of fresh root ginger, peeled and cut into fine shreds
6–8 spring onions (scallions), cut into shreds
30ml/2 tbsp light soy sauce
salt and freshly ground black pepper

1 Strip the leaves from the coriander stalks. Pile them on a chopping board and coarsely chop them.

2 Bring a large pan of lightly salted water to the boil and cook the noodles until they are just tender. Drain, rinse under cold water and drain again. Return to the clean pan and toss with 15ml/1 tbsp of the oil.

3 Preheat a wok until hot, add the remaining oil and swirl it around. Add the ginger and stir-fry for a few seconds, then add the noodles and spring onions. Stir-fry over a medium heat for 3–4 minutes, until hot.

4 Sprinkle over the soy sauce and coriander and season to taste. Toss well, transfer to a warmed bowl and serve.

Cook's Tip

Many of the dried egg noodles available are sold in skeins or bundles. As a guide, allow one skein of noodles per person as an average portion for a main dish.

SPECIAL OCCASIONS

Whether a New Year's Eve dinner or a birthday lunch, pasta is the perfect choice for a special occasion. With this sensational collection of exquisite recipes you can choose either a baked dish to prepare in advance and pop in the oven when your guests arrive or a quick-cook combination that is ready in minutes. After all, who wants to be stuck in the kitchen while everyone else is having a party? What is more, as pasta is both filling and economical, you can afford to go to town on luxurious and extravagant sauces. Spaghettini with Vodka & Caviar or Capelli d'Angelo with Lobster are sure to impress without breaking the bank. Fish and shellfish are natural partners for pasta, as both require rapid cooking, and this chapter features a stunning collection of recipes with prawns (shrimp), mussels, crab, scallops, monkfish, snapper and squid. There are some fabulous meat dishes, too, from traditional Lasagne al Forno to fashionable Tagliatelle with Bacon & Radicchio. Alternatively, celebrate the Chinese way with succulent steak or lamb noodle recipes. Food should be a feast for the eyes as well as for the taste buds and this is particularly important on special occasions. All the recipes in this chapter are sinfully tempting, from intriguing Prawn & Pasta Packets to dramatic Black Pasta with Squid Sauce and from pretty Pink & Green Farfalle to elegant Crab Ravioli.

Prawn & Pasta Packets

A quick and impressive dish, which can be prepared in advance and cooked at the last minute, this is ideal for midweek entertaining.

Serves 4

450g/1lb dried tagliatelle
150ml/ 1/4 pint/ 2/3 cup Pesto
1 garlic clove, crushed
20ml/4 tsp olive oil
750g/1 1/2lb/6 cups medium raw prawns (shrimp), peeled and deveined
120ml/4fl oz/ 1/2 cup dry white wine
salt and freshly ground black pepper

1 Preheat the oven to 200°C/400°F/Gas 6. Cut out 4 x 30cm/12in squares of baking parchment.

2 Bring a large pan of lightly salted water to the boil. Add the tagliatelle and cook for 2 minutes only, then drain and tip into a bowl. Mix with half the pesto. Put the rest of the pesto in a small bowl and stir the garlic into it.

3 Place 5ml/1 tsp olive oil in the centre of each parchment square. Pile equal amounts of pasta on top.

4 Top with equal amounts of prawns and spoon the garlic-flavoured pesto over them. Season with pepper and sprinkle each serving with 30ml/2 tbsp wine.

5 Brush the edges of the parchment lightly with water and bring them loosely up around the filling, twisting tightly to enclose. (The packets should look like money bags.)

6 Place the packets on a baking sheet. Bake for 10–15 minutes. Transfer the parcels to four serving plates. Serve immediately, allowing each person to open his or her own packet.

Cook's Tip
You can use greaseproof (waxed) paper for the packets.

Pink & Green Farfalle

In this modern recipe, pink prawns and green courgettes combine prettily with cream and pasta bows to make a delicious and substantial main course.

Serves 4

50g/2oz/ 1/4 cup butter
2–3 spring onions (scallions), very thinly sliced diagonally
350g/12oz courgettes (zucchini) thinly sliced diagonally
60ml/4 tbsp dry white wine
300g/11oz/2 3/4 cups dried farfalle
75ml/5 tbsp crème fraîche
225g/8oz/1 1/3 cups cooked peeled prawns (shrimp)
15ml/1 tbsp finely chopped fresh marjoram
salt and freshly ground black pepper

1 Melt the butter in a large, heavy pan, add the spring onions and cook over a low heat, stirring frequently, for about 5 minutes, until softened.

2 Add the courgettes, season with salt and pepper to taste and stir-fry over a medium heat for 5 minutes. Pour over the wine and let it bubble, then cover and simmer for 10 minutes.

3 Bring a large pan of lightly salted water to the boil. Add the pasta and cook until it is *al dente*.

4 Meanwhile, add the crème fraîche to the courgette mixture and simmer for about 10 minutes, until well reduced.

5 Add the prawns to the courgette mixture, heat through gently and taste for seasoning. Drain the pasta and tip it into a warmed bowl. Add the sauce and chopped marjoram and toss well. Serve immediately.

Cook's Tip
Marjoram has a special affinity with fish and shellfish. If you dislike its pungency, use flat leaf parsley instead.

Fish with Fregola

This is a cross between a soup and a stew. Serve it with crusty Italian bread.

Serves 4–6

75ml/5 tbsp olive oil
4 garlic cloves, finely chopped
½ small fresh red chilli, seeded and finely chopped
1 large handful fresh flat leaf parsley, coarsely chopped
1 red snapper, about 450g/1lb, cleaned, with head and tail removed
1 sea bass, about 500g/1¼lb, cleaned, with head and tail removed
350–450g/12oz–1lb thick cod fillet
400g/14oz can chopped tomatoes
175g/6oz/1½ cups dried fregola or any other very tiny pasta shapes, such as corallini
250ml/8fl oz/1 cup water
salt and freshly ground black pepper
ciabatta, to serve

1 Heat 30ml/2 tbsp of the olive oil in a large flameproof casserole. Add the chopped garlic and chilli, with about half the chopped fresh parsley. Fry over a medium heat, stirring occasionally, for about 5 minutes.

2 Cut all of the fish into large chunks – including the skin and the bones in the case of the snapper and sea bass – adding the pieces to the casserole as you cut them. Sprinkle the fish with a further 30ml/2 tbsp of the olive oil and fry for a few minutes.

3 Add the tomatoes, then fill the empty can with water and pour this into the pan. Bring to the boil. Season with salt and pepper to taste, stir well, lower the heat and cook, stirring occasionally, for 10 minutes.

4 Add the fregola or other pasta shapes and simmer for 5 minutes, then add the measured water and the remaining olive oil. Simmer until the pasta is *al dente*.

5 If the sauce becomes too thick, add more water, then taste for seasoning and adjust, if necessary. Serve hot in warmed bowls sprinkled with the remaining parsley and accompanied by fresh ciabatta.

Spaghetti with Bottarga

This unusual recipe, featuring salted and dried fish roe – bottarga – comes from Sardinia. It is simplicity itself to make and tastes very good.

Serves 4

350g/12oz fresh or dried spaghetti
about 60ml/4 tbsp olive oil
2–3 whole garlic cloves, peeled
60–90ml/4–6 tbsp grated bottarga, to taste
salt and freshly ground black pepper

1 Bring a large pan of lightly salted water to the boil and cook the spaghetti until it is *al dente*.

2 Meanwhile, heat half the olive oil in a separate pan. Add the garlic and cook gently, stirring, for a few minutes. Remove the pan from the heat, scoop out the garlic with a slotted spoon and discard it.

3 Drain the pasta very well. Return the pan of garlic-flavoured oil to the heat and add the pasta. Toss well, season with pepper and moisten with the remaining oil.

4 Divide the pasta among four warmed bowls, sprinkle the grated bottarga over the top and serve immediately.

Cook's Tip
You can buy bottarga, made from mullet or tuna roe, in Italian delicatessens. Small jars of ready-grated bottarga are convenient, but the best flavour comes from vacuum-packed slices of mullet bottarga. These are very easy to grate on a box grater. Keep any leftover bottarga tightly wrapped in the refrigerator, so that it does not taint other foods.

Spaghetti with Mussels

Mussels are delicious with pasta. The combination of the black shells and creamy spaghetti strands looks stylish too.

Serves 4

900g/2lb live mussels, scrubbed and bearded
250ml/8fl oz/1 cup water
400g/14oz dried spaghetti
75ml/5 tbsp olive oil
3 garlic cloves, finely chopped
60ml/4 tbsp chopped fresh parsley
60ml/4 tbsp white wine
salt and freshly ground black pepper

1 Check the mussels, discarding any which are not tightly closed or which fail to close when tapped with the back of a knife. Put them in a large heavy pan. Pour in the measured water and place the pan over a moderate heat. As soon as the mussels open, lift them out individually.

2 When all the mussels have opened (discard any that do not), pour the liquid in the pan through a strainer lined with kitchen paper and reserve until needed.

3 Bring a large pan of lightly salted water to the boil and cook the spaghetti until it is *al dente*.

4 Meanwhile, heat the oil in a large frying pan. Add the garlic and parsley and cook for 2–3 minutes. Add the mussels, their strained juices and the wine, with plenty of pepper. Heat the mixture gently, but do not let the mussels toughen.

5 Drain the pasta and return it to the clean pan. Add the sauce, and toss to coat. Serve immediately.

Cook's Tip
To clean mussels, scrub off any sand or mud under cold running water and knock off any barnacles with a knife. Pull away the beard – the tuft that protrudes from the hinge of the shell – with your fingers.

Spaghetti with Creamy Mussel & Saffron Sauce

In this recipe the pasta is tossed with a delicious pale yellow mussel sauce, streaked with yellow threads of saffron.

Serves 4

900g/2lb live mussels, scrubbed and bearded
150ml/ ¼ pint/ ⅔ cup dry white wine
2 shallots, finely chopped
450g/1lb dried spaghetti
25g/1oz/2 tbsp butter
2 garlic cloves, crushed
10ml/2 tsp cornflour (cornstarch)
300ml/ ½ pint/1 ¼ cups double (heavy) cream
pinch of saffron threads
juice of ½ lemon
1 egg yolk
salt and freshly ground black pepper
chopped fresh parsley, to garnish

1 Check the mussels, discarding any which are not tightly closed or which fail to close when tapped with the back of a knife. Put them in a large, heavy pan. Add the wine and shallots, cover and cook over a high heat, shaking the pan frequently, for about 5–10 minutes, until the mussels have opened. Discard any that remain shut.

2 Remove the mussels with a slotted spoon and pour the cooking liquid through a strainer lined with kitchen paper. Return it to the pan and boil until reduced by half. Meanwhile, reserve a few mussels and remove the rest from their shells.

3 Bring a large pan of lightly salted water to the boil, add the pasta and cook until *al dente*. Meanwhile, melt the butter in a pan, add the garlic and cook until golden. Stir in the cornflour and gradually stir in the mussel liquid and the cream. Add the saffron to the sauce, with salt and pepper to taste. Simmer until slightly thickened. Stir in lemon juice to taste, then the egg yolk and shelled mussels. Keep warm, but do not boil.

4 Drain the pasta and return it to the clean pan. Add the mussel sauce and toss. Serve in warmed bowls, garnished with the reserved mussels in their shells and the parsley.

Penne with Prawns & Artichokes

This is a good dish for late spring or early summer, when baby artichokes appear in shops and on market stalls.

Serves 4

juice of ½ lemon
4 baby globe artichokes
90ml/6 tbsp olive oil
2 garlic cloves, crushed
30ml/2 tbsp chopped fresh mint
30ml/2 tbsp chopped fresh flat leaf parsley
350g/12oz/3 cups dried penne
8–12 cooked king or tiger prawns (jumbo shrimp), peeled, deveined and each cut into 2–3 pieces
25g/1oz/2 tbsp butter
salt and freshly ground black pepper

1 Fill a medium bowl with cold water and add the lemon juice to acidulate it. (This is to prevent the cut surfaces of the artichokes from discolouring.)

2 Prepare the artichokes one at a time. Cut off the stalks, if present, and cut across the tops of the leaves. Peel off and discard any tough outer leaves. Cut the artichokes lengthways into quarters and remove the hairy chokes. Then cut the pieces of artichoke lengthways into 5mm/ ¼in slices and put these in the bowl of acidulated water as you prepare them.

3 Drain the artichoke slices and pat them dry with kitchen paper. Heat the olive oil in a frying pan and add the artichokes, garlic and half the mint and parsley. Season with salt and pepper to taste and cook over a low heat, stirring, until the artichokes feel tender when pierced with a sharp knife.

4 Meanwhile, bring a large pan of lightly salted water to the boil and cook the pasta until *al dente*. Add the prawns to the artichokes, stir thoroughly to mix, then heat through gently for 1–2 minutes.

5 Drain the pasta and tip it into a warmed bowl. Add the butter and toss until it has melted. Add the artichoke mixture and toss to combine. Serve immediately, sprinkled with the remaining herbs.

Paglia e Fieno with Prawns & Vodka

The combination of prawns, vodka and pasta may seem unusual, but it has become something of a modern classic in Italy.

Serves 4

30ml/2 tbsp olive oil
¼ large onion, finely chopped
1 garlic clove, crushed
15–30ml/1–2 tbsp sun-dried tomato purée (paste)
200ml/7fl oz/scant 1 cup panna da cucina or double (heavy) cream
350g/12oz fresh or dried paglia e fieno
12 raw tiger prawns (jumbo shrimp), peeled, deveined and chopped
30ml/2 tbsp vodka
salt and freshly ground black pepper

1 Heat the oil in a medium pan, add the onion and garlic and cook gently, stirring frequently, for 5 minutes, until softened.

2 Add the tomato purée and stir for 1–2 minutes, then add the cream and bring to the boil, stirring. Season with salt and pepper to taste and let the sauce bubble until it starts to thicken slightly. Remove from the heat.

3 Bring a large pan of lightly salted water to the boil and cook the pasta until it is *al dente*. When it is almost ready, add the prawns and vodka to the sauce; toss quickly over a medium heat for 2–3 minutes, until the prawns turn pink.

4 Drain the pasta and tip it into a warmed bowl. Pour the sauce over and toss well. Divide among four warmed bowls and serve immediately.

Cook's Tip

Make sure that the pasta has only a minute or two of cooking time left before adding the prawns (shrimp) to the sauce. Otherwise the prawns will overcook and become tough.

Linguine with Crab

This makes a rich and tasty first course or can be served for a lunch or supper with crusty Italian bread.

Serves 4

about 250g/9oz/generous 1 cup crab meat
45ml/3 tbsp olive oil
1 small handful fresh flat leaf parsley, coarsely chopped, plus extra, to garnish
1 garlic clove, crushed
350g/12oz ripe plum tomatoes, peeled and chopped
60–90ml/4–6 tbsp dry white wine
350g/12oz fresh or dried linguine
salt and freshly ground black pepper

1 Put the crab meat in a mortar and pound it to a coarse pulp with a pestle or use a sturdy bowl and a rolling pin. Set aside.

2 Heat 30ml/2 tbsp of the oil in a pan. Add the parsley and garlic, fry briefly, then stir in the tomatoes, crab meat and wine. Cover and simmer for 15 minutes, stirring occasionally.

3 Meanwhile, bring a large pan of lightly salted water to the boil and cook the pasta until it is *al dente*.

4 Drain the pasta, reserving a little of the cooking water, and return to the clean pan. Add the remaining oil and toss quickly over a medium heat until the oil coats the strands. Add the tomato and crab mixture to the pasta and toss again, adding a little of the reserved cooking water if the sauce seems too thick. Season to taste with salt and pepper. Serve hot, in warmed bowls, sprinkled with parsley.

Cook's Tip

The best way to obtain crab meat is to ask a fishmonger to remove it from the shell for you or to buy dressed crab from the supermarket. For this recipe you will need one large crab and you should use both the white and dark meat.

Crab Ravioli

This recipe for a dinner party appetizer uses chilli-flavoured pasta, which looks and tastes good with crab, but you can use plain pasta.

Serves 4

3-egg quantity Basic Pasta Dough, flavoured with 5–10ml/1–2 tsp crushed, dried red chillies
flour, for dusting
75g/3oz/6 tbsp butter
juice of 1 lemon

For the filling

175g/6oz/¾ cup mascarpone cheese
175g/6oz/¾ cup crab meat
30ml/2 tbsp finely chopped fresh flat leaf parsley, plus extra to garnish
finely grated rind of 1 lemon
pinch of crushed dried chillies
salt and freshly ground black pepper

1 Make the filling. Put the mascarpone in a bowl and mash it with a fork. Stir in all the remaining ingredients.

2 Using a pasta machine, roll out one-quarter of the pasta into a 90–100cm/36–39in strip. Cut the strip with a sharp knife into 2 x 45–50cm/18–20in lengths (you can do this during rolling if the strip gets too long to manage). With a 6cm/2½in fluted cutter, stamp out eight squares from each pasta strip.

3 Using a teaspoon, put a mound of filling in the centre of half the squares. Brush a little water around the edge of the filled squares, then top with the plain squares and press the edges to seal. Press the edges with the tines of a fork to decorate.

4 Put the ravioli on floured dishtowels, sprinkle lightly with flour and leave to dry while repeating the process with the remaining dough to make 32 ravioli altogether.

5 Cook the ravioli in a large pan of salted boiling water for 4–5 minutes. Meanwhile, heat the butter and lemon juice in a small pan until sizzling.

6 Drain the ravioli and divide among four warmed bowls. Drizzle the lemon butter over the ravioli and serve with parsley.

Fettuccine with Scallops in Tomato Sauce

Scallops have a rich yet delicate flavour and so are best combined with ingredients that will not overpower it.

Serves 4

450g/1lb dried fettuccine
30ml/2 tbsp olive oil
2 garlic cloves, finely chopped
450g/1lb shelled scallops, sliced in half horizontally
30ml/2 tbsp chopped fresh basil
salt and freshly ground black pepper
fresh basil sprigs, to garnish

For the sauce

30ml/2 tbsp olive oil
½ onion, finely chopped
1 garlic clove, finely chopped
2 x 400g/14oz cans peeled tomatoes

1 Make the sauce. Heat the oil in a large, shallow pan. Add the onion and garlic and cook for about 5 minutes, until just softened, stirring occasionally.

2 Add the tomatoes, with their can juice and crush roughly with a fork. Bring to the boil, then reduce the heat and simmer gently for 15 minutes, until thickened. Remove the pan from the heat and set aside.

3 Bring a large pan of lightly salted water to the boil. Add the pasta and cook until *al dente*.

4 Meanwhile, heat the oil in a frying pan, add the garlic and cook for about 30 seconds, until just sizzling. Add the scallops, with 2.5ml/ ½ tsp salt. Cook over a high heat for about 3 minutes, tossing the scallops until they are cooked through.

5 Reheat the tomato sauce, stir in the scallops and keep warm.

6 Drain the fettuccine, return it to the clean pan and add the scallops and tomato sauce and the chopped basil. Toss thoroughly to mix. Transfer to four warmed plates, garnish with the basil sprigs and serve immediately.

Rigatoni with Scallops & Pernod

Scallops have the sweetest flavour and need very little cooking, which makes them perfect partners for pasta.

Serves 4

350g/12oz scallops
45ml/3 tbsp olive oil
1 garlic clove, chopped
1 onion, chopped
2 carrots, cut into thin batons
350g/12oz dried rigatoni
30ml/2 tbsp chopped fresh parsley
30ml/2 tbsp dry white wine
30ml/2 tbsp Pernod
150ml/ ¼ pint/ ⅔ cup double (heavy) cream
salt and freshly ground black pepper

1 Trim the scallops, cut off the corals, then cut the scallops in half lengthways.

2 Heat the oil in a frying pan and fry the garlic, onion and carrots over a low heat for about 10 minutes, until the carrots are softened.

3 Meanwhile, bring a large pan of lightly salted water to the boil. Add the pasta and cook until *al dente*.

4 Stir the scallops, parsley, wine and Pernod into the vegetable mixture and bring to the boil. Cover, lower the heat and simmer for 1 minute. Using a slotted spoon, transfer the scallops and vegetables to a plate and keep them warm.

5 Bring the pan juices back to the boil and boil rapidly until reduced by half. Stir in the cream and heat the sauce through.

6 Stir the scallops and vegetables into the creamy sauce in the pan and heat through. Season to taste. Drain the pasta and toss it with the sauce. Serve immediately.

Cook's Tip

The key to this sauce is not to overcook the scallops, or they will become tough and rubbery.

Black Pasta with Squid Sauce

Tagliatelle flavoured with squid ink looks amazing and tastes deliciously of the sea. Marrying it with rings of fresh squid doubles the impact on the eyes and on the taste buds.

Serves 4

105ml/7 tbsp olive oil
2 shallots, chopped
3 garlic cloves, crushed
45ml/3 tbsp chopped fresh parsley
675g/1½lb prepared squid, cut into rings and rinsed
150ml/¼ pint/⅔ cup dry white wine
400g/14oz can chopped tomatoes
2.5ml/½ tsp dried chilli flakes
450g/1lb dried squid ink tagliatelle
salt and freshly ground black pepper

1 Heat the oil in a pan and add the shallots. Cook over a low heat, stirring occasionally, until pale golden, then add the garlic. When the garlic has begun to colour a little, stir in 30ml/2 tbsp of the parsley, then add the squid and stir again. Cook for 3–4 minutes.

2 Add the white wine, simmer for a few seconds, then stir in the tomatoes and chilli flakes and season with salt and pepper to taste. Cover and simmer gently for about 1 hour, until the squid is tender. Thin the sauce with a little water if necessary.

3 Bring a large pan of lightly salted water to the boil, add the pasta and cook until it is *al dente*.

4 Drain the tagliatelle and return it to the pan. Add the squid sauce and mix well. Serve in warmed bowls, sprinkled with the remaining chopped parsley.

Cook's Tip
Squid is available all year round, both fresh and frozen. You can buy it ready-prepared to save time.

Spaghetti with Squid & Peas

In Italy, squid is often cooked with peas in a tomato sauce. This recipe is a variation on the theme.

Serves 4

450g/1lb prepared squid
30ml/2 tbsp olive oil
1 small onion, finely chopped
1 garlic clove, finely chopped
400g/14oz can chopped tomatoes
15ml/1 tbsp red wine vinegar
5ml/1 tsp sugar
10ml/2 tsp finely chopped fresh rosemary
115g/4oz/1 cup frozen peas
350g/12oz fresh or dried spaghetti
15ml/1 tbsp chopped fresh flat leaf parsley
salt and freshly ground black pepper

1 Cut the squid bodies into strips about 5mm/¼in wide. Finely chop the tentacles.

2 Heat the oil in a large shallow pan, add the onion and garlic and cook gently, stirring, for about 5 minutes until softened. Add the squid, tomatoes, red wine vinegar and sugar. Stir in the rosemary, with salt and pepper to taste. Bring to the boil, stirring, then cover and simmer gently for 20 minutes.

3 Uncover the pan, add the peas and cook for 10 minutes. Meanwhile, bring a large pan of lightly salted water to the boil, add the pasta and cook until it is *al dente*.

4 Drain the pasta and tip it into a warmed serving bowl. Pour the sauce over the pasta, add the parsley, toss well and serve.

Cook's Tip
A good fishmonger will prepare squid for you, but if you do need to prepare it yourself, here's how. Holding the body in one hand, gently pull away the head and tentacles. Discard the head; chop and reserve the tentacles. Remove the transparent "quill" from inside the body. Peel off the brown skin, rub a little salt into the squid and wash under cold running water.

Spaghettini with Vodka & Caviar

This is an elegant yet easy way to serve spaghettini. Serve it for a sophisticated after-theatre supper.

Serves 4

60ml/4 tbsp olive oil
3 spring onions (scallions), thinly sliced
1 garlic clove, finely chopped
400g/14oz dried spaghettini
120ml/4fl oz/ ½ cup vodka
150ml/ ¼ pint/ ⅔ cup double (heavy) cream
75g/3oz/ ½ cup caviar
salt and freshly ground black pepper

1 Heat the oil in a small pan. Add the spring onions and garlic, and cook gently for 4–5 minutes.

2 Bring a large pan of lightly salted water to the boil. Add the pasta and cook until *al dente*.

3 Pour the vodka and cream into the spring onion mixture and cook over a low heat for 5–8 minutes.

4 Remove the vodka sauce from the heat and stir in half the caviar. Season with salt and pepper to taste.

5 Drain the pasta, return it to the clean pan and toss immediately with the sauce. Serve on warmed plates, with a little of the reserved caviar in the centre of each portion.

Cook's Tip
True caviar is salted sturgeon roe and ranges in colour from greenish grey through brown and golden to very dark grey. Red "caviar" is salmon or sea trout roe, or red-dyed lumpfish roe. This may also be dyed black. Look-alike caviars are generally saltier than the real thing.

Pasta with Prawns & Feta

This dish combines the richness of fresh prawns with the tart saltiness of feta cheese.

Serves 4

450g/1lb/4 cups dried penne, garganelli or rigatoni
50g/2oz/ ¼ cup butter
450g/1lb raw prawns (shrimp), peeled and deveined
6 spring onions (scallions), chopped
225g/8oz feta cheese, cubed
small bunch fresh chives, chopped
salt and freshly ground black pepper

1 Bring a large pan of lightly salted water to the boil. Add the pasta and cook until *al dente*.
2 Melt the butter in a frying pan and stir in the prawns. When they turn pink, add the spring onions and cook, stirring occasionally, for 1 minute. Stir in the feta and half the chives. Season to taste with pepper.
3 Drain the pasta, pile it on a warmed serving dish and top with the sauce. Sprinkle with the remaining chives and serve.

Capelli d'Angelo with Lobster

This is a sophisticated, stylish dish for an extra-special occasion.

Serves 4

meat from the body, tail and claws of 1 cooked lobster
juice of ½ lemon
40g/1½ oz/3 tbsp butter
4 fresh tarragon sprigs, leaves stripped and chopped
60ml/4 tbsp double (heavy) cream
90ml/6 tbsp sparkling dry white wine
60ml/4 tbsp fish stock
300g/11oz fresh capelli d'angelo
salt and freshly ground black pepper
about 10ml/2 tsp lumpfish roe, to garnish (optional)

1 Cut the lobster meat into small pieces and put it in a bowl. Sprinkle with the lemon juice.

2 Melt the butter in a large pan, add the lobster meat and tarragon and stir over the heat for a few seconds.

3 Pour in the cream and stir for a further few seconds, then add the sparkling wine and stock and season with salt and pepper to taste. Simmer for 2 minutes, then remove from the heat and cover.

4 Bring a large pan of lightly salted water to the boil and cook the pasta until it is *al dente*. It will require only a few minutes. Drain well, reserving a few spoonfuls of the cooking water.

5 Place the pan of lobster sauce over a medium to high heat, add the pasta and toss for just long enough to combine and heat through, moistening with a little of the reserved water from the pasta. Serve immediately in warmed bowls and sprinkle each portion with lumpfish roe if you like.

Variation
Make the sauce with Champagne rather than sparkling white wine, if you are planning to serve Champagne with the meal.

Monkfish & Prawn Lasagne

Rich and creamy, this flavoursome lasagne makes a good supper-party dish.

Serves 6

65g/2½oz/5 tbsp butter
450g/1lb monkfish fillets, skinned and diced
225g/8oz raw prawns (shrimp), peeled and deveined
225g/8oz/3 cups button (white) mushrooms, chopped
40g/1½oz/⅓ cup plain (all-purpose) flour
600ml/1 pint/2½ cups hot milk
300ml/½ pint/1¼ cups double (heavy) cream
400g/14oz can chopped tomatoes
30ml/2 tbsp shredded fresh basil
8 sheets no-precook lasagne
75g/3oz/1 cup freshly grated Parmesan cheese
salt and freshly ground black pepper
fresh herbs, to garnish

1 Melt 15g/½oz/1 tbsp of the butter in a large pan, add the monkfish and prawns and sauté for 2–3 minutes. When the prawns turn pink, transfer the fish and prawns to a bowl.

2 Add the mushrooms to the pan and sauté for 5 minutes. Remove with a slotted spoon and add to the fish in the bowl.

3 Melt the remaining butter in the pan, add the flour and cook for 1 minute. Gradually add the milk, stirring until the sauce boils and thickens. Whisk in the cream and cook over a low heat for 2 minutes more. Remove the sauce from the heat and stir in the fish and mushroom mixture with all the juices that have collected in the bowl. Season to taste. Preheat the oven to 190°C/375°F/Gas 5.

4 Spread half the chopped tomatoes over the bottom of an ovenproof dish. Sprinkle with half the basil and season to taste. Ladle one-third of the fish sauce over the tomatoes. Cover with four lasagne sheets. Spread the remaining tomatoes over and sprinkle with the rest of the basil. Ladle another third of the sauce over. Top with lasagne, spread the remaining sauce over and cover with the cheese. Bake for 30–40 minutes, until golden and bubbling. Serve hot, garnished with fresh herbs.

Shellfish Lasagne

This is a luxury lasagne perfect for a special occasion meal.

Serves 4–6

4–6 scallops, with corals
450g/1lb raw tiger prawns (jumbo shrimp), peeled and deveined
1 garlic clove, crushed
75g/3oz/6 tbsp butter
50g/2oz/½ cup plain (all-purpose) flour
600ml/1 pint/2½ cups hot milk
100ml/3½ fl oz/scant ½ cup double (heavy) cream
100ml/3½ fl oz/7 tbsp dry white wine
2 sachets of saffron powder
good pinch of cayenne pepper
130g/4½ oz Fontina cheese, thinly sliced
75g/3oz/1 cup freshly grated Parmesan cheese
6–8 sheets fresh egg lasagne
salt and freshly ground black pepper

1 Preheat the oven to 190°C/375°F/Gas 5. Cut the scallops, corals and prawns into bitesize pieces and spread them in a dish. Sprinkle with the garlic and season to taste. Melt about one-third of the butter in a pan and toss the shellfish over a medium heat for 1–2 minutes, or until the prawns turn pink. Remove with a slotted spoon and set aside.

2 Melt the remaining butter in the pan. Add the flour and cook for 1 minute. Gradually add the hot milk, stirring constantly until the sauce boils and becomes very thick and smooth.

3 Whisk in the cream, wine, saffron powder and cayenne and season with salt and pepper to taste, then remove the sauce from the heat.

4 Spread one-third of the sauce over the bottom of an ovenproof dish. Arrange half the Fontina slices over and sprinkle with one-third of the grated Parmesan. Scatter half the shellfish evenly on top, then cover with half the lasagne sheets. Repeat the layers, then cover with the remaining sauce and Parmesan.

5 Bake the lasagne for 30–40 minutes, or until the topping is golden brown and bubbling. Allow to stand for 10 minutes before serving.

Rigatoni with Pork

This is an excellent meat sauce using pork rather than the more usual beef.

Serves 4

25g/1oz/2 tbsp butter
30ml/2 tbsp olive oil
1 small onion, finely chopped
½ carrot, finely chopped
½ celery stick, finely chopped
2 garlic cloves, crushed
150g/5oz minced (ground) pork
60ml/4 tbsp dry white wine
400g/14oz can chopped Italian plum tomatoes
a few fresh basil leaves, plus extra, to garnish
400g/14oz/3½ cups dried rigatoni
salt and freshly ground black pepper
freshly shaved Parmesan cheese, to serve

1 Heat the butter and oil in a large pan until just sizzling, add the chopped vegetables and garlic, and cook over a medium heat, stirring frequently, for 3–4 minutes.

2 Add the minced pork and cook gently for 2–3 minutes, breaking up any lumps in the meat with a wooden spoon. Fry for 2–3 minutes more.

3 Stir in the wine, tomatoes, basil leaves, salt to taste and plenty of pepper. Bring to the boil, then lower the heat, cover and simmer for 40 minutes, stirring occasionally.

4 Bring a large pan of lightly salted water to the boil and cook the pasta until it is *al dente*. Just before draining it, add one to two ladles of the cooking water to the sauce. Stir well.

5 Drain the pasta, add it to the pan of sauce and toss well. Serve, sprinkled with the basil and shaved Parmesan.

Variation
To give the sauce a more intense flavour, soak 15g/½oz dried porcini mushrooms in 175ml/6fl oz/¾ cup warm water for 15–20 minutes, then drain, chop and add with the meat.

Pork Meatballs with Pasta

Serve these tasty meatballs on a bed of spaghetti.

Serves 6

450g/1lb lean minced (ground) pork
1 leek, finely chopped
115g/4oz/3 cups mushrooms, finely chopped
15ml/1 tbsp chopped fresh thyme
15ml/1 tbsp tomato purée (paste)
1 egg, beaten
30ml/2 tbsp plain (all-purpose) flour
oil, for frying the meatballs
500g/1¼lb dried spaghetti
salt and freshly ground black pepper
fresh thyme sprigs, to garnish

For the tomato sauce
15ml/1 tbsp olive oil
1 onion, finely chopped
1 carrot, finely chopped
1 celery stick, finely chopped
1 garlic clove, crushed
675g/1½ lb ripe tomatoes, peeled, seeded and chopped
150ml/¼ pint/⅔ cup dry white wine
150ml/¼ pint/⅔ cup well-flavoured vegetable stock
15ml/1 tbsp tomato purée (paste)
15ml/1 tbsp chopped fresh basil

1 Preheat the oven to 180°C/350°F/Gas 4. Put the pork, leek, mushrooms, chopped thyme, tomato purée, egg and flour in a bowl and stir together until thoroughly mixed. Shape into small balls, place on a plate, cover and chill.

2 Make the tomato sauce. Heat the olive oil in a frying pan and fry the onion and carrot until softened. Add all the remaining sauce ingredients, season to taste, then bring to the boil. Boil, uncovered, for 10 minutes, until thickened.

3 Heat the oil in a frying pan, add the meatballs in batches and cook until lightly browned. Using a slotted spoon, place them in a shallow, ovenproof dish and pour the tomato sauce over. Cover and bake for about 1 hour, until cooked through.

4 Bring a pan of lightly salted water to the boil and cook the pasta until *al dente*. Drain, divide among warmed bowls, spoon in the meatballs and sauce and garnish with thyme sprigs.

Tagliatelle with Bacon & Radicchio

This modern recipe is deliciously rich, and makes a good dinner-party first course or, served with salad, an excellent lunch dish.

Serves 4

225g/8oz dried tagliatelle
75–90g/3–3$\frac{1}{2}$oz pancetta or rindless streaky (fatty) bacon, diced
25g/1oz/2 tbsp butter
1 onion, finely chopped
1 garlic clove, crushed
1 head of radicchio, about 115–175g/4–6oz finely shredded
150ml/ $\frac{1}{4}$ pint/ $\frac{2}{3}$ cup double (heavy) cream
50g/2oz/ $\frac{2}{3}$ cup freshly grated Parmesan cheese
salt and freshly ground black pepper

1 Bring a large pan of lightly salted water to the boil and cook the tagliatelle until it is *al dente*.

2 Meanwhile, put the pancetta or bacon in a medium pan and heat gently until the fat runs. Increase the heat slightly and stir-fry the pancetta or bacon for 5 minutes.

3 Add the butter to the pan. When it melts, add the onion and garlic, and stir-fry for 5 minutes. Add the radicchio and toss for 1–2 minutes until wilted.

4 Pour in the cream, add the grated Parmesan and season with salt and pepper to taste. Stir for 1–2 minutes, until the cream is bubbling and the ingredients are evenly mixed.

5 Drain the pasta and tip it into a warmed bowl. Pour the sauce over and toss well. Serve immediately.

Cook's Tip

Italian cooks use radicchio di Treviso, which has long, pointed leaves that are dramatically striped in dark red and white, but other varieties, such as Castelfranco, may also be used. Sadly, they all lose their lovely red colouring when cooked.

Penne with Pancetta & Cream

This makes a gloriously rich supper dish. The egg yolks are lightly cooked on contact with the hot pasta.

Serves 3–4

300g/11oz/2$\frac{3}{4}$ cups dried penne
30ml/2 tbsp olive oil
1 small onion, finely chopped
175g/6oz dried pancetta
1–2 garlic cloves, crushed
5 egg yolks
175ml/6fl oz/ $\frac{3}{4}$ cup double (heavy) cream
115g/4oz/1$\frac{1}{3}$ cups grated Parmesan cheese, plus extra to serve
salt and freshly ground black pepper

1 Bring a large pan of lightly salted water to the boil and cook the penne until *al dente*.

2 Meanwhile, heat the oil in a separate large pan and cook the onion over a low heat, stirring frequently, for about 5 minutes, until soft and translucent.

3 Add the pancetta and garlic. Cook over a medium heat until the pancetta is cooked but not crisp.

4 Put the egg yolks in a jug (pitcher) and add the cream and Parmesan. Grind in plenty of pepper and beat well to mix.

5 Drain the penne thoroughly, tip into the pan containing the pancetta mixture and toss over a high heat to mix. Remove the pan from the heat and immediately pour in the egg yolk mixture, tossing well to combine. Spoon into a large, shallow serving dish, grind a little extra black pepper over and sprinkle with some of the extra Parmesan. Serve immediately, with the rest of the Parmesan.

Cook's Tip

Use free-range eggs from a reputable source. Having added the egg yolks, don't return the pan to the heat or the egg yolks will scramble and spoil the appearance of the dish.

Lasagne al Forno

The classic lasagne is great for a special-occasion meal.

Serves 6

45ml/3 tbsp olive oil
500g/1¼ lb lean minced (ground) beef
75g/3oz diced pancetta
130g/4½ oz chicken livers, trimmed and chopped
1 onion, finely chopped
2 garlic cloves, crushed
150ml/ ¼ pint/ ⅔ cup dry white wine
30–45ml/2–3 tbsp tomato purée (paste)
2 x 400g/14oz cans chopped tomatoes
45ml/3 tbsp single (light) cream
about 8–10 fresh lasagne sheets, green or white, precooked if necessary
75g/3oz/1 cup freshly grated Parmesan cheese
salt and freshly ground black pepper
fresh flat leaf parsley sprigs, to garnish

For the white sauce

600ml/1 pint/2½ cups milk
1 bay leaf
1 small onion, sliced
50g/2oz/ ¼ cup butter
40g/1½oz/ ⅓ cup plain (all-purpose) flour
freshly grated nutmeg

1 Heat the oil in a large pan. Add the beef and brown, breaking it up with a wooden spoon. Add the pancetta and chicken livers and cook for 3–4 minutes. Add the onion and garlic and cook for 5 minutes. Stir in the wine and cook until reduced.

2 Stir in the tomato purée and tomatoes, and season with salt and pepper to taste. Bring to the boil, then lower the heat and simmer for 15–20 minutes, until thickened. Stir in the cream, remove from the heat and set aside.

3 Meanwhile, make the white sauce. Pour the milk into a pan, and add the bay leaf and onion. Heat until the milk is just below boiling point, then remove the pan from the heat and leave to infuse (steep) for 10 minutes. Scoop out the bay leaf and onion.

4 Melt the butter in a pan and stir in the flour. Cook for 1 minute, stirring constantly, then gradually whisk in the milk until the mixture boils and thickens to a smooth sauce. Season and add nutmeg to taste.

5 Preheat the oven to 190°C/375°F/Gas 5. Spread some meat sauce on the bottom of a rectangular ovenproof dish. Top with a layer of lasagne. Trickle over some white sauce and sprinkle with Parmesan. Repeat the layers, finishing with a layer made by swirling the last of the two sauces together. Sprinkle liberally with grated Parmesan.

6 Bake the lasagne for about 30 minutes, until bubbling and golden brown. Allow to stand for 10 minutes before cutting. Serve garnished with flat leaf parsley.

Cook's Tip

There's no need to spread out the white sauce – just add it in generous spoonfuls. When you add the sheets of lasagne, press down evenly and the sauce will spread naturally.

New York-style Lasagne

This sophisticated lasagne is made by layering the meat sauce with ricotta, spinach and pepperoni.

Serves 6

400g/14oz fresh spinach
about 8–10 lasagne sheets, green or white, precooked if necessary
125g/4oz thinly sliced pepperoni sausage
500g/1¼ lb/2½ cups ricotta cheese, mashed with a fork
50g/2oz/ ⅔ cup freshly grated Parmesan cheese

For the meat sauce

30ml/2 tbsp olive oil
250g/9oz minced (ground) beef
250g/9oz minced (ground) pork
1 onion, chopped
2 garlic cloves, crushed
60ml/4 tbsp dry vermouth
400g/14oz can chopped tomatoes
45ml/3 tbsp tomato purée (paste)
150ml/ ¼ pint/ ⅔ cup beef stock or water
2.5ml/ ½ tsp dried oregano
salt and freshly ground black pepper

1 Snap off any thick stalks from the spinach, then blanch the leaves in a little boiling water until just wilted. Drain and refresh under cold water. Drain again, squeeze dry and chop the leaves.

2 Make the meat sauce. Heat the oil in a large frying pan, add the minced meats and cook over a high heat, stirring to break up any lumps, for about 5 minutes, until well browned. Add the onion and garlic and cook for 5 minutes more.

3 Add the vermouth and cook over a high heat until reduced. Stir in the remaining sauce ingredients. Bring to the boil, then lower the heat and simmer for 20–30 minutes, until thickened.

4 Preheat the oven to 190°C/375°F/Gas 5. In a large ovenproof dish, layer the meat sauce with the pasta sheets, chopped spinach and sliced sausage. Dot each layer of spinach and sausage with the ricotta and sprinkle with the Parmesan. Finish with a generous topping of Parmesan.

5 Bake for 35–40 minutes, until bubbling and golden. Leave to stand for 10 minutes before serving.

Sicilian Lasagne

In Sicily, their lasagne is traditionally made with pork rather than beef.

Serves 6

45ml/3 tbsp olive oil
1 small onion, finely chopped
½ carrot, finely chopped
½ celery stick, finely chopped
250g/9oz boneless pork
60ml/4 tbsp dry white wine
400ml/14fl oz/1⅔ cups passata (bottled strained tomatoes)
200ml/7fl oz/scant 1 cup chicken stock
15ml/1 tbsp tomato purée (paste)
2 bay leaves, torn
15ml/1 tbsp chopped fresh flat leaf parsley
250g/9oz fresh lasagne sheets
2 hard-boiled (hard-cooked) eggs, sliced
125g/4½ oz mozzarella cheese, drained and sliced
60ml/4 tbsp freshly grated Pecorino cheese
salt and freshly ground black pepper

1 Heat 30ml/2 tbsp of the oil in a large pan and cook the chopped vegetables over a medium heat, stirring frequently, for about 10 minutes.

2 Add the pork and fry until well browned all over. Pour in the wine and let it bubble and reduce for a few minutes, then add the passata, stock, tomato purée and bay leaves, with the parsley and salt and pepper to taste. Mix well, cover and cook, stirring occasionally, for 30–40 minutes, until the pork is tender.

3 Using a slotted spoon, remove the bay leaves and meat. Discard the bay leaves. Chop the meat and return it to the pan.

4 Preheat the oven to 190°C/375°F/Gas 5. Bring a pan of lightly salted water to the boil. Cut the lasagne sheets into 2.5cm/1in strips and add to the water. Cook for 3–4 minutes until just *al dente*. Drain well, then stir the strips into the sauce.

5 Spoon half the pasta and sauce mixture into a shallow ovenproof dish. Cover with half the egg and mozzarella slices and half the Pecorino. Repeat the layers, drizzle the remaining oil over and bake for 30–35 minutes, until golden and bubbling.

Lamb & Sweet Pepper Sauce

Not a speedy pasta dish – the sauce needs to be cooked for about an hour – but well worth waiting for.

Serves 4–6

60ml/4 tbsp olive oil
250g/9oz boneless lamb neck (shoulder) fillet, diced
2 garlic cloves, finely chopped
2 bay leaves, torn
250ml/8fl oz/1 cup dry white wine
4 ripe plum tomatoes, peeled and chopped
2 large red (bell) peppers, seeded and diced
350–425g/12–15oz dried maccheroni alla chitarra or any long macaroni
salt and freshly ground black pepper

1 Heat half the olive oil in a flameproof casserole, add the lamb and sprinkle with a little salt and pepper. Cook the meat over a medium to high heat, stirring frequently, for about 10 minutes, until the pieces of meat are browned on all sides.

2 Sprinkle in the garlic and add the bay leaves, then pour in the wine and let it bubble until reduced.

3 Stir in the remaining olive oil, with the tomatoes and the red peppers. Cover and simmer over a low heat, stirring occasionally, for 45–55 minutes, or until the lamb is very tender.

4 Bring a large pan of lightly salted water to the boil and cook the pasta until it is *al dente*.

5 Drain the pasta well and return it to the clean pan. Remove the bay leaves from the sauce, then add the sauce to the pasta, toss well and serve immediately.

Cook's Tips
• The (bell) peppers don't have to be red. Use yellow, orange or green if you like; either a single colour or a mixture.
• If you need to add water to the sauce towards the end of cooking, take it from the pan used for cooking the pasta.

Cantonese Fried Noodles

A crisp crust of fried noodles is topped with beef and stir-fried vegetables.

Serves 2–3

25g/1oz Chinese dried mushrooms
225g/8oz dried egg noodles
60ml/4 tbsp vegetable oil
225g/8oz lean steak, sliced into thin strips
1 leek, trimmed and sliced into thin batons
225g/8oz can bamboo shoots, drained and sliced into thin batons
150g/5oz Chinese leaves (Chinese cabbage), cut into small diamond shapes
15ml/1 tbsp cornflour (cornstarch)
15ml/1 tbsp rice wine or dry sherry
30ml/2 tbsp dark soy sauce
5ml/1 tsp sesame oil
5ml/1 tsp caster sugar

1 Soak the dried mushrooms in a small bowl of warm water for 30 minutes. Meanwhile, bring a pan of lightly salted water to the boil and cook the noodles until tender. Drain, rinse under cold water and drain again. Pat dry with kitchen paper.

2 Drain the mushrooms, reserving 90ml/6 tbsp of the soaking water. Cut off and discard the stems, then slice the caps thinly.

3 Heat half the oil in a large frying pan and sauté the noodles lightly. Press them against the base of the pan until they form a flat, even cake. Cook for 4 minutes, or until crisp underneath, then slide the noodle cake on to a plate. Invert it and return it to the pan. Cook for 3 minutes more, then slide on to the plate again and keep hot.

4 Preheat a wok and add the remaining oil. When hot, stir-fry the beef, mushrooms, leek and bamboo shoots for 2–3 minutes. Add the Chinese leaves and stir-fry for 1–2 minutes.

5 Put the cornflour in a bowl and stir in the reserved soaking water to make a paste. Add to the wok with the remaining ingredients and cook for 15 seconds to thicken. Divide the noodles among two to three warmed bowls and pile the stir-fried mixture on top.

Braised Birthday Noodles with Hoisin Lamb

It is considered bad luck to cut birthday noodles since this might shorten one's life.

Serves 4

350g/12oz thick dried egg noodles
1kg/2¼ lb neck (shoulder) fillets of lamb
30ml/2 tbsp vegetable oil
15ml/1 tbsp cornflour (cornstarch)
30ml/2 tbsp soy sauce
30ml/2 tbsp rice wine
grated rind and juice of ½ orange
15ml/1 tbsp hoisin sauce
15ml/1 tbsp wine vinegar
5ml/1 tsp light brown sugar
115g/4oz fine green beans
salt and freshly ground black pepper
2 hard-boiled (hard-cooked) eggs, halved, and 2 spring onions (scallions), finely chopped, to garnish

For the marinade

2 garlic cloves, crushed
10ml/2 tsp grated fresh root ginger
30ml/2 tbsp soy sauce
30ml/2 tbsp rice wine
1–2 dried red chillies
30ml/2 tbsp vegetable oil

1 Bring a large pan of lightly salted water to the boil. Add the noodles and cook for 2 minutes only. Drain, rinse under cold water and drain again. Set aside.

2 Cut the lamb into 5cm/2in thick medallions. Mix the ingredients for the marinade in a large shallow dish. Add the lamb and leave to marinate for at least 4 hours or overnight.

3 Heat the oil in a heavy pan. Drain the lamb, reserving the marinade, and fry until browned on all sides. Pour over the marinade and add just enough water to cover. Bring to the boil, skim, then lower the heat and simmer for 40 minutes, or until the meat is tender, adding more water as needed.

4 Mix the cornflour, soy sauce, rice wine, orange rind and juice, hoisin sauce, vinegar and sugar. Stir into the lamb. Add the noodles and beans. Simmer until cooked. Season. Divide among four bowls, garnish with half an egg and spring onions. Serve.

Index

A
Anchovies: cannelloni Sorrentina-style, 51
chilli, anchovy & tomato pasta, 34
macaroni with anchovies & mixed vegetables, 34
orecchiette with anchovies & broccoli, 32
pasta with spinach & anchovy sauce, 32
Arugula *see* Rocket

B
Bacon: pasta with fresh tomato & smoky bacon sauce, 39
piquant penne with chillies &, 57
pumpkin, bacon & Parmesan pasta, 57
spaghetti with onion &, 39
spätzle, 56
stir-fried bacon & pak choi with pasta, 39
tagliatelle with radicchio &, 90
Bamie goreng, 45
Beef: Bolognese sauce, 58
Cantonese fried noodles, 93
Corsican beef stew with macaroni, 62
lasagne al forno, 91
New York-style lasagne, 91
pastitsio, 62
simple baked lasagne, 60

tagliatelle with meat sauce, 58
three-cheese lasagne, 60
Bolognese sauce, 58
Bottarga, spaghetti with, 81
Bread: garlic breadcrumbs, 57
Bucatini, 8
with raw tomato sauce, 68
Bucatoni, 8
Buckwheat noodles: chicken & buckwheat noodle soup, 21

C
Campanelle, 9
Cannelloni, 10
Sorrentina-style, 51
with tuna, 51
Cantonese fried noodles, 93

Capelli, 8
Capelli d'angelo, 8
with lobster, 87
Caviar, spaghettini with vodka &, 87
Cellophane noodles, 11
fried, & prawns 47
prawn noodle salad with fragrant herbs, 28
Cheat's lasagne with mixed mushrooms, 74
Cheese: baked macaroni cheese, 73
creamy pasta with Parmesan curls, 71
macaroni with four cheeses, 73
ravioli with four cheese sauce, 76
spicy cheese lasagne, 76
summer salad with pasta, 27
Chiang Mai noodle soup, 21
Chickpea soup with ditalini, 17
Chicken: bamie goreng, 45
broccoli & chicken lasagne, 53
chicken & broccoli salad, 26
chicken & buckwheat noodle soup, 21
chicken & pasta balti, 38
chicken & pepper pasta salad, 26
chicken pasta salad, 26
chicken soup with noodles, 20
Chinese chicken with cashew nuts, 63
egg noodle salad with sesame chicken, 28
farfalle with cherry tomatoes &, 54
farfalle with sausage &, 53
fusilli with tomato sauce &, 38
gingered chicken noodles, 63
pappardelle with mushrooms &, 54
rich minestrone, 19
special fried noodles, 45
see also Liver
Chinese chicken with cashew nuts, 63
Chitarra, 8
Chow mein: shellfish, 46
Clams: spaghetti with red wine clam sauce, 36
tagliolini with clam, leek & tomato sauce, 36
Conchiglie, 9
with chicken livers & herbs, 52
with roasted vegetables, 70
Conchiglione, 10
Consommé with agnolotti, 16
Cooking pasta, 13
Corsican beef stew with macaroni, 62

Country pasta salad, 27
Courgettes (zucchini): courgette soup with pastina, 18
Crab: crab ravioli, 84
linguine with, 84
Creamy pasta with Parmesan curls, 71

E
Egg noodles, 11
Eggs: vermicelli frittata, 70
Eliche, 9

F
Farfalle, 9
pink & green, 80

with chicken & cherry tomatoes, 54
with chicken & sausage, 53
with prawns, 35
with tuna, 33
Fettuccine, 8
all'Alfredo, 71
bolognese with baby tomatoes, 61
with scallops in tomato sauce, 85
Fidelini, 8
Filled pasta, 10
Fiorelli, 9
Fish soup, Provençal, 16
Fish with fregola, 81
Frittata, vermicelli, 70
Fusilli, 9
with chicken & tomato sauce, 38
with wild mushrooms & herbs, 69
Fusilli lunghi, 8

G
Garganelli, 9
Garlic: garlic breadcrumbs, 57
spaghetti olio e aglio, 66
spaghettini with garlic & chilli oil, 66

H
Haddock: tagliatelle with avocado & haddock sauce, 50
Ham: linguine with smoked ham & artichokes, 40
prosciutto pasta with asparagus, 40
spaghetti with saffron &, 43
tagliatelle with leeks & prosciutto, 41
tortellini with, 43
warm pasta salad with, 25
Herbs: herb pasta, 12

J
Japanese summer salad, 29

L
Lamb: braised birthday noodles with hoisin lamb, 93
lamb & sweet pepper sauce, 92
Lasagne, 10
al forno, 91
broccoli & chicken, 53
cheat's lasagne with mixed mushrooms, 74
flavoured lasagne, 10
monkfish & prawn, 88
New York-style, 91
shellfish, 88
Sicilian, 92
simple baked lasagne, 60
spicy cheese, 76
three-cheese, 60
Lasagnette, 10
Linguine, 8
with crab, 84
with pesto, 67
with smoked ham & artichokes, 40
Little stuffed hats in broth, 18
Liver: conchiglie with chicken livers & herbs, 52
tagliatelle with aubergines & chicken livers, 52
Lobster, capelli d'angelo with, 87
Long pasta, 8
Loopy noodle nests, 77
Lumaconi, 10

M
Macaroni, 8
baked macaroni cheese, 73
Corsican beef stew with, 62
lamb & sweet pepper sauce, 92
pastitsio, 62
with anchovies & mixed vegetables, 34
with four cheeses, 73
Meatballs: pork meatballs with pasta, 89
Mediterranean salad with basil, 22
Minestrone, 19
Monkfish & prawn lasagne, 88
Mushrooms: cheat's lasagne with, 74
fusilli with wild mushrooms & herbs, 69
pasta with sun-dried tomatoes &, 69
spirali with wild mushrooms & chorizo sauce, 42
Mussels: spaghetti with creamy mussel & saffron sauce, 82
spaghetti with mussels, 82

N
New York-style lasagne, 91
Noodles, 11
bamie goreng, 45
braised birthday noodles with hoisin lamb, 93
Cantonese fried noodles, 93
Chiang Mai noodle soup, 21
chicken soup with, 20
Chinese chicken with cashew nuts, 63
egg noodle salad with sesame chicken, 28
gingered chicken noodles, 63
loopy noodle nests, 77
seafood chow mein, 46
sesame noodle salad, 29
soft fried noodles, 77
special fried noodles, 45
Thai fried noodles, 47

tossed noodles with seafood, 46
with ginger & coriander, 77
see also Buckwheat noodles; Cellophane noodles; Soba noodles; Somen noodles; Vermicelli

O
Orecchiette, 9
with anchovies & broccoli, 32
with prawns & feta, 87

P
Paglia e fieno, 72
Pancetta: penne with cream &, 90
spaghetti with two-way tomatoes &, 56
Pappardelle, 8
with chicken & mushrooms, 54
Pasta: basic dough, 12
with fresh tomato and smoky bacon sauce, 39
with mushrooms & sun-dried tomatoes, 69
with prawns & petits pois, 35

with spinach & anchovy sauce, 32
Pasta machines, 12
Pasta, types of, 8–10
Pastina, 10
Pastitsio, 62
Peas: fresh pea & ham soup, 17
paglia e fieno, 72
Penne, 9
piquant with bacon & chillies, 57
with pancetta & cream, 90
with prawns & artichokes, 83
with salame Napoletano, 42
Pepperoni pasta, 44
Pesto: linguine with, 67
Pink & green salad, 24
Pipe, 9
Pipe rigate, 9
Pork: pork meatballs with pasta, 89
rigatoni with, 89
Sicilian lasagne, 92
Prawns (shrimp): farfalle with, 35
fried cellophane noodles, 47
paglia e fieno with vodka &, 83
pasta with feta &, 87
pasta with petits pois &, 35
penne with artichokes &, 83
pink & green farfalle, 80
pink & green salad, 24
prawn & pasta packets, 80
prawn noodle salad with fragrant herbs, 28
Thai fried noodles, 47
Prosciutto: pasta with asparagus, 40
tagliatelle with leeks &, 41
tagliatelle with Parmesan &, 41
see also Ham
Provençal fish soup with pasta, 16
Pumpkin: pumpkin & spaghetti soup, 18
pumpkin, bacon & Parmesan pasta, 57

R
Ravioli, 13
crab ravioli, 84
spinach & dolcelatte ravioli, 75
with four cheese sauce, 76
with Swiss chard, 75
Rice noodles, 11
Rice vermicelli *see* Vermicelli
Rich minestrone, 19
Rigatoni, 9
with pork, 89
with scallops & Pernod, 85
with spicy sausage and tomato sauce, 44
with tomato & tuna sauce, 50
Rocket: spaghetti with rocket pesto, 67
Rotelle, 9
Ruote, 9

S
Salami *see* Sausage
Sardinian sausage & pasta, 59
Sausage: pasta salad with salami & olives, 25

penne with salame Napoletano, 42
rigatoni with spicy sausage & tomato sauce, 44
Sardinian sausage & pasta, 59
tortiglioni with salami, 59
Scallops: fettuccine with scallops in tomato sauce, 85
rigatoni with Pernod &, 85
shellfish lasagne, 88
tagliatelle with brandied scallops, 37
warm scallop & conchiglie salad, 23
Seafood: seafood chow mein, 46
seafood laksa, 20
seafood salad, 24
tossed noodles with seafood, 46
Sesame noodle salad, 29
Shaping pasta, 13
Short pasta, 9
Shrimp see Prawns
Sicilian lasagne, 92
Smoked salmon: smoked salmon & dill pasta salad, 23

warm smoked salmon & pasta salad, 23
Soba noodles, 11
Somen noodles, 11
Japanese summer salad, 29
Thai noodle salad, 29
Spaghetti, 8
pork meatballs with pasta, 89
pumpkin & spaghetti soup, 18
spaghetti olio e aglio, 66
spaghetti tetrazzini, 55
squid ink pasta with ricotta, 37
three tomato Bolognese, 58
turkey & pasta bake, 55

warm smoked salmon & pasta salad, 23
with bacon & onion, 39
with bottarga, 81
with creamy mussel & saffron sauce, 82
with fresh tomato sauce, 68
with ham & saffron, 43
with mussels, 82
with pancetta & two-way tomatoes, 56
with red wine clam sauce, 36
with rocket pesto, 67
with squid & peas, 86
with tuna & anchovies, 33
spaghettini, 8
with garlic & chilli oil, 66
with vodka & caviar, 87
Spätzle, 56
Spinach: pasta with spinach & anchovy sauce, 32
spinach & dolcelatte ravioli, 75
spinach pasta, 12
Spirali, 9
with wild mushrooms & chorizo sauce, 42
Squid: black pasta with squid sauce, 86
spaghetti with peas &, 86
Squid ink pasta with ricotta, 37
Strangozzi, 8
Strozzapreti, 9
Summer salad with pasta, 27
Swiss chard, ravioli with, 75

T
Tagliarini, 8
with white truffle, 74
Tagliatelle, 8, 13
black pasta with squid sauce, 86
paglia e fieno, 72
prawn & pasta packets, 80
prosciutto pasta with asparagus, 40
pumpkin, bacon & Parmesan pasta, 57
warm pasta salad with ham, 25
with aubergines & chicken livers, 52
with avocado & haddock sauce, 50
with baby vegetables, 72
with bacon & radicchio, 90
with Bolognese sauce, 61
with brandied scallops, 37
with leeks & prosciutto, 41
with meat sauce, 58
with prosciutto & Parmesan, 41
with prosciutto & peppers, 41
Tagliolini, 8
with clam, leek & tomato sauce, 36
Thai fried noodles, 47
Thai noodle salad, 29
Tomatoes: bucatini with raw tomato sauce, 68
spaghetti with fresh tomato sauce, 68
three tomato Bolognese, 58
tomato pasta, 12
Tortellini, 13
with ham, 43
Tortiglioni with salami, 59
Truffles: tagliarini with white truffle, 74
Tuna: cannelloni with, 51
farfalle with, 33
Mediterranean salad with basil, 22
rigatoni with tomato & tuna sauce, 50
spaghetti with anchovies &, 33
tuna pasta salad, 22
Turkey: spaghetti Tetrazzini, 55

turkey, mushroom & pasta bake, 55

U
Udon noodles, 11

V
Vegetables: conchiglie with roasted vegetables, 70
tagliatelle with baby vegetables, 72
Vermicelli, 8, 11
seafood laksa, 20
vermicelli frittata, 70

W
Wholemeal pasta, 12

Z
Ziti, 8
Zucchini see Courgettes